Trivia by the Dozen

Trivia by the Dozen

Encouraging Interaction and Reminiscence in Managed Care

by Jean Vetter

Venture Publishing, Inc.
State College, Pennsylvania

Production Manager: Richard Yocum
Manuscript Editing: Valerie Fowler, Richard Yocum, Christina Manbeck

Library of Congress Catalogue Card Number 2007923911
ISBN-10   1-892132-68-0
ISBN-13   978-1-892132-68-0

Dedicated to my friend and mentor

Janice Booth

with thanks for
your teaching, your wisdom, your love of the language and
for never letting your students give less than their best.

Table of Contents

Introduction

I firmly believe that advancing years and health issues cannot diminish a person's need to have fun, to interact with others, and to reminisce about special times.

People can't be lonely or depressed when they are actively involved in discussions about things that are important to them. As activity directors, staff members and volunteers, we need to be mindful that everyone in a managed care situation was once a powerful and independent person. They were parents, bosses, professionals, and skilled workers. We must give all of them opportunities to remember and talk, and to never let go of their sense of worth.

Many years ago when I first started volunteering in a nursing home, the activity director assigned me to help a particularly difficult gentleman with his craft project. The more he struggled to twist his pipe cleaners into a chicken shape, the more frustrated he became until he finally threw them at the table—and missed.

I didn't know how to respond, so I jokingly said, "I bet you used to be a baseball pitcher." He frowned a moment, then he said proudly, "No, I made custom jewelry." The hands that he could no longer control had once created fine, beautiful things. As I gradually gained his confidence and we tried other activities, it became clear that he excelled at word games. Nobody could beat him at trivia, so we played word games to use his strengths."

I wrote *Trivia by the Dozen* to encourage people in managed care to use those strengths. It is a collection of questions divided into categories of things that were fundamental to clients' lives during their most productive years. There are no trick questions and no science or math questions that might intimidate shy or slower players. Songs, movies, clothing, household items, and world events that were important to individuals when they were independent are used to help stimulate memories. These can be a catalyst for vibrant dialogue.

Each game consists of twelve questions, a number small enough to enable clients with limited endurance or a short attention span to play without taxing their strength. The familiar themes will help awaken recollections of happy times, thereby setting the stage for the discussion questions that follow.

All Dressed Up

1. Short, layered ballet skirt.

2. Nun's dress.

3. Pleated, heavy collar.

4. Pad worn at back of skirt under the waist.

5. Circular frame worn under a long skirt.

6. Protective garment worn by chefs and blacksmiths.

7. Loose Japanese robe fastened by sash.

8. Julius Caesar wore one of these loose, flowing garments. What was it?

9. Dancers, acrobats and gymnasts wear a close-fitting garment called what?

10. One end of this piece of cloth falls to the feet, the other end goes over a Hindu lady's shoulder.

11. A bride traditionally wears this garment to signify modesty.

12. This is worn by doctors and nurses.

Answers on page 113

Let's Talk

- Clothing is often designed to meet people's needs. Discuss the reasons why the following garments were invented: armor, helmet, spacesuit, wetsuit, bulletproof vest.

- Some clothing is worn strictly by women, some by men, but one kind of casual pants (jeans) is worn equally by men and women, kids and adults. Do you remember when women first started wearing jeans? How long did you resist before you accepted the practice?

- Hats were once standard articles of clothing. Men never left home without one, and women were never seen in church without one. Do you still wear a hat regularly? Does a hat make you feel more dressed up? Do you even own a hat?

All Dressed Up Bonus Questions

1. Short coverings designed to be worn over shoes, and fastened underneath by a strap.

2. A protective cloth tied under a baby's chin.

3. A form-fitting, sleeveless garment worn under a suit jacket.

4. Cold weather shoes with runners attached to the bottom.

5. Trousers, full at the thigh and close-fitting from the knee to the ankle, often worn at fox hunts.

6. A plastic garment circled by elastic and used to protect hair from water.

7. Elastic or leather straps designed to support trousers.

8. Footless, tubular garments worn by dancers on their calves.

9. A garment worn by infants is changed frequently. What is it?

10. A skin-tight garment worn by divers in cold waters to retain body heat.

11. Baseball shoes known by an attachment on the sole.

12. A folded cloth worn tied around the head.

Answers on page 113

Angels

1. What is the primary ingredient in an angel food cake?

2. One old adage says "Fools rush in where angels...

3. What is the name given to a celestial being that has been assigned to protect a mortal?

4. There was an all-black 332nd Fighter Group that trained at Tuskegee, Alabama, in World War II, and painted their plane tails vermilion. What nickname did this earn them?

5. In the Gospel of Luke, an archangel appeared to Mary to announce that she would bear a child? What was the archangel's name?

6. If seraphim are the highest order of angels, what is the name given to the angels that are one grade below them?

7. When Jesus was seized at Gethsemane, he told his captors that he could pray and his Father would give more than how many legions of angels?

8. An old expression meant to insult a woman was call her a street angel but a house...

9. An early gangster movie starring James Cagney, Pat O'Brien, and The Dead End Kids tells the story of two friends who grow up—one to be a gangster and one a priest.

10. If a business or a play is said to have an angel, it means somebody is contributing...

11. Complete this line from a song by Johnny Mercer and Ziggy Elman that was introduced in the musical *Dream*: "We kiss, and the angels..."

12. Michael Shaara's Pulitzer Prize-winning novel *Killer Angels* gives a detailed account of what great battle that took place on American soil?

Answers on page 113

Let's Talk

• When you very young, did anybody ever call you a "little angel?" If so, did that say something about the kind of child you were? How would you say you usually behaved? If you were too full of mischief to be called angelic, what were some of the things you did?

• Was there ever a time in your life when you believed that you had a guardian angel caring for you? Tell the group about why you thought so.

• Why do people often refer to babies as "angels" but they very seldom say it about people when they get older?

Animal Friends

1. A wild dog that is native to Australia howls, yelps, crows and purrs, but rarely barks. Name this dog.

2. An elephant is a very large animal, with very large body parts. What is the part of the elephant that can weigh up to 300 pounds?

3. We call turkeys "gobblers" because of the sound they make. However, only about half of all turkeys can actually gobble. Which ones mostly make a clicking sound instead?

4. Some people are afraid of bats because of their rodent-like appearance. However, a bat's appetite for eating mosquitoes actually makes it a good friend to man. How many mosquitoes can a bat eat in an hour?

5. What mammals are known to live longer than any other mammal on earth?

6. This is the world's largest nonflying bird and it has a powerful kick. What is it?

7. What fish swims in huge schools that have been known to attack animals as large as horses?

8. What creature is helpful to the farmer because it digs tunnels that allow water and oxygen to reach the roots of plants?

9. What bird is capable of flying backward?

10. Hornets make paper by mixing wood pulp with what?

11. What male fish carry the female's eggs in a kangaroo-like pouch until they hatch?

12. Hemophilia is treated by a medicine that is made from the venom of what reptile?

Answers on page 113

Let's Talk

- How many people here have had an unusual animal as a pet? What was it? What were some of its characteristics?

- Describe an interesting or memorable thing your pet once did.

- What kind of animal do you think is best-suited for people who live in apartments or small homes, and what kind is more appropriate on a farm? Why do you think so?

Animals Getting Together

1. A group of toads together are said to be a knot. What do you call it when a great group of geese are gathered?

2. If you see multiple monkeys swinging socially through the sumac, what are they called?

3. What do you call a big bunch of bees?

4. A parade of prancing ponies would be called what?

5. Several fish swimming together are said to be in what?

6. What are copious cattle grazing in the grass called?

7. What do you call lots of lions?

8. Harness a few oxen together and what do you have?

9. If you see a bevy of bears, just call them a…

10. Umpteen elephants would be called what?

11. Gnats and grasshoppers gathering together actually look like what they are called. What is it?

12. Seals and whales are called the same thing when they are seen simultaneously. What is it?

Answers on page 113

Let's Talk

- You may have had a cat that gave birth to adorable and cute kittens. Did you know that a litter of kittens is called a kindle (or an intrigue)? What did you do with the babies?

- Did you or your children ever raise a school of tropical fish for fun or profit? If so, did the entire family become experts?

- Ask people in the group to name other groups of animals. Have them tell about the largest animal groups they have ever encountered and explain how they came to see them.

Bad Guys and Gals

1. After the murder of her parents, legend grew up around the daughter. People said that she "took an ax and gave her mother forty whacks." Who was she?

2. A really bad couple, whose last names were Parker and Barrow, were bank robbers and killers of 14 people. How did the newspapers popularly refer to them?

3. Another bad guy from the 1930s, George was a man who kidnapped, murdered and robbed banks. He was so handy with a Tommy gun he could write his name in bullets. Who was he?

4. Charles Arthur was this bad boy's first and middle names. His nickname described his youthful, extremely handsome face. The nickname was paired with his last name, and that's the name we remember. Who was he?

5. One doting mother of four believed in family togetherness, so she engaged her boys in the family business, which consisted of murder, kidnapping, and robbery. Who was this notorious 1930s mom?

6. The FBI actually put out a "Wanted Dead or Alive" poster on the first man they called Public Enemy Number One. He met his end in a hail of bullets while coming out of a movie theater in Chicago. Who was he?

7. This criminal, Lester M. Gillis, had several aliases including George Nelson and Jimmy Williams. His small stature and his face like an innocent child belied the work he did as a gunman for Dillinger. Who was this bad guy?

8. A husband and wife who were convicted of espionage and executed in 1953 proclaimed their innocence to the end. Who were they?

9. Name the German immigrant who was convicted for the kidnapping and murder of the Lindbergh baby, and was subsequently executed in 1936.

10. William H. Bonney was born in Brooklyn but moved away from home and became one of the Old West's most famous outlaws. What is the nickname that identifies the young man to this day?

11. Caril Ann Fugate was the teenager who joined her boyfriend in a vicious killing rampage in the 1950s. Who was her murderous partner in crime?

12. The flamboyant criminal known as Scarface is said to have ordered the famous St. Valentine's Day Massacre. What was this bad guy's name?

Answers on page 113

Let's Talk

• Why do you suppose so many people have gone afoul of the law, when statistics have proven that crime does not pay?

• Was there ever a person in your hometown who earned the dubious reputation of being a really bad person? Tell us about it.

• Was anybody in this room ever involved in law enforcement? Tell the group what your job was and how you came to do that work.

Begins With "be"

1. To act a certain way.

2. To mislead or trick.

3. To resent another person for owning something.

4. Start.

5. To be indebted.

6. A living person is a human.

7. Earlier.

8. To do something in my interest is to do it on my what?

9. Leave.

10. Not in front.

11. A command.

12. Look.

Answers on page 114

Let's Talk

- Add the prefix "be" to the following words and make a sentence with them: devil, fog, labor, little, numb, neath, witch.

- A wounded Clint Eastwood is taken to recuperate in a girls' school in the South during the Civil War in the 1971 movie *The Beguiled*. Does anybody remember what happened to him there?

- When kids are asked why they did something, they often answer, "Because." Did you ever respond that way? Did it seem a good reason at the time? Have you used that explanation as an adult? When?

Begins With "em"

1. To hire.

2. Dorothy lived with her auntie… in Kansas.

3. To show strong feeling by acting in an exaggerated manner.

4. A bright green precious stone used in jewelry.

5. A person who leaves his country to settle in another does what?

6. While speaking, you put special force on a word. What is it called?

7. You work for someone else. What are you called?

8. The glass has nothing in it. It is…

9. A type of ornamental needlework.

10. What is it called when a person has money entrusted to his care, then steals it?

11. A big hug.

12. An Australian bird that can't fly, but its running speed makes up for that lack.

Answers on page 114

Let's Talk

- Ask everybody to say a word starting with "em" and use it in a sentence.

- Emily is a female name that is spelled differently in different countries. The Latin spelling is Emile, meaning excellent. Emilie is German, Emilia is Italian, both meaning industrious. The masculine form is Emil. Is there an Emily or an Emil in this group?

- Emily Dickinson was a Massachusetts girl who wrote poetry in the 19th century. She was so private that of the 1,800 poems she wrote, only seven were published in her lifetime. Is anybody here familiar with her poetry? Does anybody write poetry?

Black

1. What country singer/songwriter was sometimes called "The Man In Black" because he wore only black clothing when he performed?

2. What is another name for a small club with a flexible handle?

3. Sorcery that is used for evil purposes is also known by another name. What is it?

4. A person with wicked intentions is said to be what?

5. A person who loses consciousness is said to suffer a what?

6. A workman who makes horseshoes is called what?

7. Name the spider with the hourglass-shaped mark on its body whose female is notorious for killing the male after mating.

8. A region in space whose gravitational field is so intense that nothing can escape is called what?

9. If a person's name is added to a list that is used to keep him from membership or employment, he is said to be on a what?

10. What is a person called who disgraces his family?

11. The bruising in the optical area as a result of a blow to the face is called what?

12. A common wildflower with yellow petals and a nearly black center is known as what?

Answers on page 114

Let's Talk

• When a person is not cheerful, he is said to be in a "black mood." Why do you suppose the color black is associated with lack of cheer?

• Men's tuxedos are traditionally black. What reasons can you give for men not wearing bright colored suits for formal wear?

• The "little black dress" has always been considered a safe choice for a woman to wear to a sophisticated event. Discuss why this is true.

Blue

1. Something coming from out of the blue is regarded as what kind of event?

2. Diana Ross and Billy Dee Williams starred in a 1972 movie biography about Billie Holiday. What was the title?

3. What is the name of the violet-blue color that is often used as a dye?

4. If Frank Sinatra had been teaching a class in loneliness when he sang "You'll walk the floor and you'll wear out your shoes," what would his students have been there for?

5. The blues seem to be rough on shoes. Hank Williams sings about going to a dance where he wore his out too. He woke up the next day wishing he could lose something. What was it?

6. Neil Diamond was a teacher too when he told us to "take the blues and sing 'em out again." What was the title of his catchy hit song?

7. Even the breeze in the trees must have been blue when it started singing weird melodies—in what classic blues song?

8. There is a famous painting by Sir Thomas Gainsborough showing a young boy in a very fancy suit. What is the title of the painting?

9. Marlene Dietrich became a huge international star by playing a cruel nightclub vixen named Lola-Lola in what 1930 movie?

10. Bonnie Blue Butler was a baby girl born to a very famous couple in literature. Who were her parents?

11. Dan Aykroyd and John Belushi played a couple of zany musicians on TV's "Saturday Night Live," then turned the act into a successful movie. What stage name did they use?

12. The dark marbling in blue cheese is actually what?

Answers on page 114

Let's Talk

• Imagine you are looking out of your hotel window at an ocean beach. Name everything you can see that is blue.

• Now imagine you are walking through a large zoo. How many animals can you see that are blue in color?

• You were just awarded a blue ribbon in a contest. The person who gave it to you is said to have blue blood. What place did you win? What does blue blood mean?

Body Parts

1. From earliest times, one body part was believed to be the center of human affection? What part was it?

2. Dogs, or canines, bear little similarity to humans, but the human body does have a canine. Where is it located?

3. What do dentists stress as the single most important way to help protect your teeth so that you may keep them as long as possible?

4. We all know how important it is to be able to breathe. Where does the respiratory system begin?

5. Each of the many organs in the human body has a specific job to do to keep the body functioning efficiently. What is the body's largest organ?

6. What is considered to be the normal temperature of the human body?

7. We use the same word to describe a certain type of needlework that we use when we talk about the body repairing a bone. What is the word?

8. George Kennedy won a Best Supporting Actor Oscar for a prison film with Paul Newman in 1967, but a reference to a card game gave Newman his nickname and the movie its title. Name the body part and the movie.

9. What is the word that describes an addition at the end of a book, as well as a part of the human large intestine?

10. The prow of a ship is also referred to as what human body part?

11. You just revealed someone's identity to the police. There is a slang expression that says that you put one of your body parts on the suspect. What part is it?

12. A host often sits at this table position, identified by this body part.

Answers on page 114

Let's Talk

- TV commercials deal with countless products aimed at improving parts of our bodies. Why is that true?

- All of our faces are different and easily recognized. But if a friend's face is in shadow, how many of his other body parts are distinctly individual enough to be identified?

- Because we need all of our body parts, science has developed some useful replacements for people who need them. Name some of the parts that can successfully be replaced.

Bookish Words

1. A paper you put in a book to keep your place.

2. Your matches are secured inside a cardboard folder. What do you call it?

3. The guy you give your money to when you bet on the horses.

4. You store your books neatly on a...

5. Someone who studies a lot.

6. A person who is extremely fond of reading is said to be...

7. A vehicle that serves as a traveling library.

8. The person hired to handle a company's ledgers.

9. The supports placed on each side of a row of books to hold them upright.

10. To make an engagement or to reserve a room.

11. A printed label, usually denoting ownership, inside the cover of a book is called what?

12. A person who binds books by trade is called a...

Answers on page 114

Let's Talk

- Some people make their living analyzing books and writing book reviews. Would you be inclined to buy a book that had been given an unfavorable review?

- There are many kinds of books. Name some. (Hints: cookbooks, encyclopedias, dictionaries, romance novels)

- What is your favorite kind of book? Do you have a favorite author? Discuss your reading preferences.

Bridges

1. The bridge in the title of Simon and Garfunkel's 1970 hit song symbolizes strength, loyalty, hope and a promise to be a friend in need. What is the title?

2. When you alienate somebody, or when you cut off any possibility of retreat in a situation, you are said to have done what?

3. A dental bridge is a mounting that connects false teeth to what?

4. One human body part has a bony upper portion called a bridge. What part of the body is it?

5. What bridge was hailed as the "Eighth Wonder of the World" when it was first spanned New York's East River in 1883?

6. The Golden Gate Bridge was the world's longest suspension bridge until 1964, when another bridge surpassed it. What is that newer bridge, located in New York Harbor?

7. William Holden was a Navy flyer co-starring with Grace Kelly in a 1954 Korean War film based on a James Michener novel. What was the title?

8. Clint Eastwood and Meryl Streep gave mid-life crisis a whole new meaning when they starred in a 1995 movie with what famous bridges in its title?

9. Alec Guinness starred in a World War II movie that won seven Oscars. Mention the film's name and somebody will probably start whistling "The Colonel Bogey March." What was this bridge and movie?

10. What bridge, finished in 1927 over the Niagara River, joining the United States and Canada, stands as a symbol of international friendship?

11. Bridge is a card game derived from this four-player card game.

12. A bridge on a musical instrument is used to raise what?

Answers on page 115

Let's Talk

- Why are armies asked to break their stride when crossing a bridge on foot? (Marching in step causes the bridge to sway, possibly weakening its structure.)

- Discuss the logic behind the old-fashioned practice of building covered bridges.

- Some highway departments place signs near bridges that say, "Bridge May Freeze First." Why would that happen?

Celebrity Quotes

What celebrity is credited with the following quotes?

1. "I am as strong as a bull moose."

2. "Let us never negotiate out of fear, but let us never fear to negotiate."

3. "It ain't over till it's over."

4. "In spite of everything I still believe that people are really good at heart."

5. Who instructed his men to "act first, talk afterward?"

6. "As I would not be a slave, so I would not be a master."

7. "People have got to know whether their president is a crook. Well, I am not a crook."

8. "Never in the field of human conflict was so much owed by so many to so few."

9. "Winning isn't everything. It's the only thing."

10. "Anybody who hates children and dogs can't be all bad."

11. "Float like a butterfly, sting like a bee."

12. "You don't understand. I could have had class. I could have been a contender. I could have been somebody, instead of a bum…which is what I am. Let's face it."

Answers on page 115

Let's Talk

- Quoting famous people plays a large part in our conversations. Where do we get some of our quotes?

- Do you have any favorite quotes that you use occasionally?

- Not all people who have influenced our thinking have been famous. Do you find yourself quoting your father or your mother? Give some examples.

Chapels and Places of Worship

1. An ancient structure in the heart of Rome has been used for religious services, a fortress, and as a site for gladiator games. What is it?

2. What is a church called if it has been built in the shape of a cross?

3. What church has been the setting for every British coronation since 1066?

4. The wedding of Prince Charles to Princess Diana took place in another famous church in London. What was it?

5. The ceiling of a chapel in the Vatican is treasured for its priceless paintings by Michelangelo. Name the chapel.

6. A small brown church in Nashua, Iowa, closes every service with a song written about it. Its original members couldn't afford paint, and it remains brown out of tradition. Name the song?

7. In Agra, India, the Shah Jahan built a gleaming marble shrine and mosque in 1646 to honor his deceased wife. What is the name of it?

8. Ivan the Terrible built a 16th century cathedral in Red Square, Moscow. Its onion domes and turrets make it one of Russia's most famous tourist attractions. What is the cathedral?

9. A Spanish mission in San Antonio was built to Christianize the Indians. Today it stands as a shrine to Texas liberty, for reasons unrelated to its original purpose. Do you remember the name of this church?

10. Patrick Henry made his famous "Give Me Liberty or Give Me Death" speech in a little white church on a hilltop in Richmond. What church was it?

11. Name the location inside a house of worship where holy writings are read.

12. The Dixie Cups made it to the top 10 in 1964 when they sang about where they intended to go and get married. Where was it?

Answers on page 115

Let's Talk

• Is there a church, synagogue, or mosque that is especially meaningful to you and your family? Where is it? Why is it important to you?

• Every culture through the ages has constructed places to worship. Why do people need a special place to pray?

• Some of the world's oldest buildings are churches. Why have they lasted when other buildings have crumbled?

Comic Strip Characters

1. Julie Newmar played a gorgeous foe of Batman on his TV show. What was her character?

2. Al Capp originated what backwoods mountain man who lived in Dogpatch? Who was this comic strip hero?

3. What was the name of a zany red-headed bird that was the star of an animated cartoon created by Walter Lantz?

4. Dagwood Bumstead overslept a lot, which drove his boss to distraction. Who was his boss?

5. Clark Kent was an unremarkable man who worked as a reporter. What was the name of his newspaper?

6. A woman reporter did not particularly respect Clark Kent, but she would gladly have flown away in the arms of his other identity, Superman. What was her name?

7. Chester Gould created a comic strip detective with an angular face and a black hat. Name the character.

8. Tess Trueheart was engaged to a comic strip detective for 18 long years before she finally managed to get him to marry her. Who was this foot-dragging gumshoe?

9. A very sassy comic strip duck liked to wear a sailor suit. What was his name and the names of his three nephews?

10. The beautiful Diana Prince was a superhero who wore bullet-repelling bracelets made from a metal found in only one place on earth—Paradise Island. Who was she?

11. Peter Parker lived happily with his Aunt May and his Uncle Ben until a radioactive insect bit him and turned him into a superhero. Who did he become?

12. Millionaire Bruce Wayne was the secret identity of what comic book hero?

Answers on page 115

Let's Talk

• Why do so many people like comic book heroes?

• Can you recall the plot of any of the comic book episodes? If the superhero won in a battle against the villain, how did he manage to do it?

Comparisons To Animals

Animal traits are sometimes used to describe people, and not always in a flattering way. Here are a few of those expressions. Different people may have heard these expressions said in different ways, so there are no really wrong answers.

1. A person who leads someone else into a trap, or someone who turns in a friend.

2. Someone who lacks courage.

3. A stupid person.

4. Someone who loves to read.

5. Quitting a habit all at once.

6. A malicious or spiteful person.

7. A glutton, a selfish person.

8. Someone who moves fast is said to be as quick as a…

9. Someone who moves slowly is said to be…

10. A person who never forgets is said to have the memory of an…

11. An unbending person is said to be as stubborn as a…

12. A fearless person is said to be as brave as a…

Answers on page 115

Let's Talk

- "Mean as a Dog." "Faithful as a Dog." "Loyal as a Dog." Are any or all of these expressions correct? Give an example of a dog you know that fits one of these sayings.

- Has anybody ever paid you a compliment by using an animal trait to describe you? How about, "Graceful as a Cat" or "Quiet as a Mouse?" What did you think about it?

- Talk about some of the animal comparisons you have heard. How were they used? Should all of them be discontinued, or are some accurate or flattering?

Comparisons To Animals Bonus Questions

1. A person who moves easily through the water is said to swim like a…

2. It's an insult to a person's intelligence to say that he has the brain of a…

3. A compliment to a person's running speed is to say that she is as fleet as a…

4. Saying that someone is "as nervous as a… in a roomful of rockers" means she is really nervous.

5. We would all like to have people think we are as wise as an...

6. Somebody who is really angry is said to be as mad as a wet...

7. A person who accomplishes a lot is said to be as busy as a...

8. You might say that someone with no scruples is as low as a...

9. One compliment for an adorable baby is to say "She's as cute as a..."

10. An idea that has long passed its worth is said to be as dead as a...

11. One way to say someone is totally contented would be to say he's as happy as a... in mud.

12. It's not a particularly flattering comparison, but you could also say someone is as contented as a... chewing her cud.

Answers on pages 115–116

Couples

1. Harriet was a big band singer. Her husband was a big band leader and his name is usually paired with hers. One of their sons became a teenage idol. Who was the father and who was the son?

2. We aren't sure whether The Lone Ranger had a wife, but another person's name comes to mind when we think of him. Who was his partner?

3. If Roy Rogers was king of the cowboys, his wife must have been queen of the cowgirls. Who was she?

4. Calamity Jane is said to have been in love many times, but she wanted one man in particular to tame her. Who was he?

5. Joanne Woodward is the lady lucky enough to not just work with, but to marry, a blue-eyed movie star. Name him.

6. Barbie is a fashion plate who probably loves clothes just a little more than she loves her boyfriend, but his name is always paired with hers. Who is he?

7. Popeye's first love was spinach, and his ladylove was next in line. Who was she?

8. They came from a large family of singers, but their television show made this brother and sister act household names from 1976–1979. Who was the duet that was "a little bit country and a little bit rock and roll"?

9. The Flintstones were a prehistoric couple with a pet dinosaur. The caveman was Fred. Name his cavewoman.

10. Lewis was half of a couple of explorers in the early 1800s. Their expedition took them from St. Louis to the Pacific Ocean, and back again. Who was his partner?

11. Robin Hood robbed the rich and gave to the poor, but he didn't try to give away a certain lady. Who was she?

12. Before Jane had a son that she called Boy, she was swinging through the jungle with one special strong man. Who was he?

Answers on page 116

Let's Talk

• Not all couples are famous. Start with your earliest memories and name some family members who come to mind in pairs.

• We've mentioned only a dozen "couples" by name. Everybody here knows countless people who are usually mentioned together. Take turns and name some of them.

• The couples mentioned in this quiz all complement each other. Take any of them and talk about whether they would have been as successful alone.

Creepy, Crawly Bugs

1. A tiny bug caused tremendous slowdown of the building of the Panama Canal. What was it?

2. One small bug lives in the American deserts. Her favorite meal is a fine dinner of her mate after mating. What is she called?

3. One rounded, flying, brightly spotted beetle is useful because it eats aphids.

4. There is a very shrill-sounding insect that appears only once every 17 years. What is it?

5. A wingless insect that lives in colonies has a highly developed social organization. Perhaps to prove it is sociable, it loves to go to picnics.

6. There is an insect that mothers of school kids hate, because it attaches itself to their children, even the cleanest ones. What is it?

7. If mothers hate lice, pet owners hate another insect with equal passion. What is it?

8. One household pest is related to grasshoppers and crickets and has existed for 250 million years. This bug prefers the nighttime, runs fast and has long feelers. Once established in a home, it's tough to get rid of it.

9. This bug loves your house so much he actually eats it. What is this wood-munching pest?

10. Hotel owners have the same feeling about a certain reddish-brown insect that mothers and pet owners have for lice and fleas. Its presence in their bedding and carpets could ruin their business.

11. Bedding and carpets are favorite hiding places for another bug that is only 1/50 of an inch long. People who suffer from allergies always try to eliminate it. What is it?

12. What is the branch of science that deals with the study of insects?

Answers on page 116

Let's Talk

- Everybody has a bug story. Share your favorite one with the group.

- Besides the fact that they are pests, why do people try to control bugs?

- Nature has provided its own brand of bug extermination. Name some natural ways insects are controlled.

Dan and Danny and Daniel

1. Name the harness race horse that never lost a race.

2. This comedian raised money to build St. Jude Children's Research Hospital in Memphis, Tennessee, in gratitude for his success.

3. "Old Dan and I with throats burned dry" is a line from what cowboy song?

4. Burt Reynolds played a detective in a 1970s TV series with the word Dan in the title. What show was it?

5. Stephen Hill played an agent named Dan in the first season of the TV series *Mission Impossible.* What was his character's last name?

6. *The Jumping Frog of Calaveras County* was named Dan'l. What beloved American author created him?

7. *Danny Boy* was the theme song of what TV show?

8. "Daniel, my brother, you are older than me," is a line from a hit song *Daniel* recorded by what bespectacled Englishman?

9. Which red-headed comedian named Danny starred in the 1952 movie *Hans Christian Andersen*?

10. What Danny is shorter than the average man, but stands tall as an actor and director? He went from starring in TV's *Taxi* to roles in many movies.

11. King Nebuchadnezzar had three men thrown into a fiery furnace for not worshiping him. Name the book of the Bible where this story appears.

12. King Darius of the Bible punished Daniel for disobeying a law, and had him thrown into a very dangerous place. What place was it?

Answers on page 116

Let's Talk

- A famous frontiersman named Daniel Boone has gone from being part of history to part of American folklore, thanks partly

to a TV show about him. Discuss the show and why you think
it was so successful.

- Dan Rather reported world events to us for many years as a TV
  newsman. Can you remember one news story he reported that
  stands out in your memory? Why?

- The song *Danny Boy* has been recorded by numerous singers.
  There are several stories about how it came to be. One says a
  father is singing about his son lost in a war. Ask everybody to
  recite lines they remember from the song. The director could
  write down the words, then have somebody read them as a poem.

Dancing

1. You don't need a partner, but you do need good abdominal
   muscles to do this exotic Middle Eastern dance, which is
   sometimes called the Oriental dance. What is it?

2. Chubby Checker didn't need a partner either, to start a dance
   craze that swept the nation in 1962. What was it?

3. Shoes with metal plates are worn when doing an extremely
   athletic dance. It can be done solo or with a partner or in a
   group. What is it?

4. You will need a partner to do the American folk dance sometimes called "hillbilly tap dancing." The shuffling of one "floor"
   foot is what distinguishes this dance from actual tap dancing.
   What is it?

5. Katharine Hepburn once summarized this famous dancing
   duo's appeal this way: She gives him sex and he gives her
   class. To whom was she referring?

6. Missionaries crossed the Pacific into present-day Hawaii to
   spread Christianity. They censured native island people for their
   culture and banned their ancient dance. What dance was it?

7. Where else except at a dance would anybody follow a singer's
   command to put one body part after another into a circle of
   people then shake it all around? What dance is it?

8. This 1977 ABBA song about a girl who was "young and sweet and
   seventeen" swept the world and remains popular today.

9. A Native American woman, Maria Tallchief, whirled to fame by performing a certain type of dance. What was it?

10. It takes four couples do a certain American folk dance. The women wear ruffled petticoats and a caller tells them what steps to take. What is the dance?

11. Michael Flatley, who calls himself "The Lord of the Dance," was born in Detroit, Michigan. He does a precise type of step-dancing. Where did it originate?

12. Greek dancers form an open circle and hold cloth squares as they leap high off the floor and spin. What is this dance?

Answers on page 116

Let's Talk

• Most cultures have a native dance that is passed down through generations. Were you taught a traditional dance in your family?

• When music plays, do you start to tap your toes and sway to the rhythm? What is your favorite type of dance music?

• On what occasions of your life has dancing played an important and memorable part?

Devils

1. These are small whirlwinds, seen on hot, dry days, and they usually contain sand and dirt particles.

2. The Cisco Kid rode a horse whose name is the Spanish word for Devil. What was his horse called?

3. A person who behaves in a reckless way, not heeding the consequences is said to have what kind of attitude?

4. Who is the ruler of evil, the prince of darkness, Satan?

5. What is the little body of land off French Guiana that was once used as a penal colony?

6. The octopus and large ray fish fall into what category of marine life?

7. A person who is mischievous, impish, malicious, and challenging is sometimes referred to as what?

8. A person who takes the unpopular side in an argument is sometimes called what?

9. Who is the Roman Catholic official whose job it is to find reasons against a candidate achieving sainthood?

10. Theodore Roosevelt dedicated this place as the first national monument in America. It is in Wyoming, near Yellowstone Park. What is it called?

11. What purple-hooded comic strip character owned a pet wolf named Devil?

12. Finish this Bible saying: When Peter urged Jesus to refuse his fate, Jesus responded by saying, "Get thee…"

Answers on page 116

Let's Talk

•   What are some other words or phrases that contain the word "devil"?

•   Why do you suppose that devil suits have always been popular as Halloween costumes among children? Do you think kids really want to be that bad?

•   What is the psychological reason sports teams often use the word "devil" in their team names?

Dogs

1. One United States sentry dog saw action in World War II, was awarded a Silver Star for his courage, and a Purple Heart for his wounds in battle. What was this hero's name?

2. A lovable cartoon-strip beagle enjoys lying on top of his little red doghouse while he pretends to be a flying ace fighting the Red Baron. What is his name?

3. A team of sled dogs ran through a blizzard in 1925 with a supply of diphtheria serum. Their noble race against the elements prevented an epidemic among the Eskimos. Name the lead dog.

4. What was the name of the dog owned by Mr. Magoo, the nearsighted cartoon character?

5. *The Call of the Wild* is a book written by Jack London, in which the hero of the story is a dog, half St. Bernard and half sheepdog. What is the dog's name?

6. President Nixon made an impassioned speech in which he used the name of his daughters' dog. What was the name of that dog?

7. The American Kennel Club classifies dogs by size. How do they refer to the smallest dogs?

8. One line from a children's nursery rhyme says, "Hi-ho, The Derry-o, The nurse takes the dog." Name that nursery rhyme.

9. When you talk about dogs, you can call them him or her. What president actually named his beagles Him and Her?

10. President Gerald Ford must have been feeling patriotic when named his golden retriever. What did he call the dog?

11. Disney made a full-length animated cartoon about two adorable dogs. One was refined female and the other was a ruffian male. Name the movie.

12. Sgt. Preston of the Yukon had a beautiful husky that led his dog team. What was the dog's name?

Answers on pages 116–117

Let's Talk

• Did you ever own a dog? How long did you have it? What was its name?

• Why do some people believe that a dog is the most loyal friend a man can have? Do you have any firsthand experience examples to prove that?

• There are many breeds of working dogs. Try to remember all of the kinds of work that man has taught dogs to do.

Ends With "ate"

1. Emphasize.

2. Adapt.

3. Settle a dispute.

4. Rejoice.

5. Pay, make amends.

6. Confuse.

7. Corrupt.

8. Sympathize.

9. Focus.

10. Connect.

11. Unite.

12. Overwhelm.

    Answers on page 117

Let's Talk

- When you were a child you were immunized against certain diseases. There is a word ending in "ate" that describes the procedure: inoculate. Do you remember your reaction when you were standing in line to get your shots? Talk about it.

- Some verbs are formed by adding "ate" to a noun, such as "assassinate" from "assassin" or by dropping the "e" first, such as "chlorinate" from "chlorine." Try to think of more.

Ends With "ate" Bonus Questions

1. Move up, adapt.

2. Destroy.

3. Adorn, embellish.

4. To assign.

5. To train.

6. Release from bondage.

7. Go to another country.

8. Fade, vanish.

9. Attract, mesmerize.

10. Reach an agreement by discussion.

11. Point out.

12. Outline.

Answers on page 117

Ends With "ute"

1. Calculate.

2. Pretty.

3. Savage.

4. Rope fiber.

5. Unspeaking.

6. Hairy.

7. Stringed instrument.

8. Unlimited, unconditional.

9. Argument.

10. Wind instrument.

11. Severe.

12. Clever.

Answers on page 117

Let's Talk

• Can you think of any more words ending in "ute?" Take a moment and name them.

• Now take the words that you thought of that end in "ute" and give synonyms for them. Use them in sentences.

• Would you enjoy reading or hearing the news if the writers did not try to use synonyms? Sportscasters try hard to not repeat words. "Run" is a word that they change, using "dash, hustle, rush, dart, scurry, sprint, and scamper." Think of a word used in your favorite sport and substitute some words for it.

Ends With "ute" Bonus Questions

1. Road, highway.

2. Greet, welcome.

3. Befoul.

4. Travel.

5. To regard or consider.

6. Appoint as agent.

7. Reduce, weaken.

8. To carry out.

9. Bring suit against.

10. Complicated.

11. 60 seconds.

12. Exceedingly small.

Answers on page 117

Family Names

1. What was the family name of *The Beverly Hillbillies?*

2. The parents of Dennis the Menace were Alice and Henry. What was their family name?

3. Mary Tyler Moore had a successful television series using her own first name. What was her family name in the show?

4. Marlon Brando was head of a large crime family in the movie *The Godfather.* What was the family name?

5. What was the name of the family in the TV series *Leave it to Beaver?*

6. Adam, Hoss and Little Joe were the sons of Ben in *Bonanza.* What was their family name?

7. Robert Reed and Florence Henderson married and combined two families of three kids each into one bunch, with the family name of...

8. Ralph and Alice were *The Honeymooners.* What was their family name?

9. The Kramden's good friends were Ed and Trixie. What was their family name?

10. What was the family name of the TV family headed by Desi Arnaz and Lucille Ball?

11. Danny Thomas starred in the TV show *Make Room for Daddy.* What was his family name in that series?

12. Shirley Jones headed a brood of talented children in a popular TV series. What was their family name?

Answers on page 117

Let's Talk

• Explain the popularity of family shows on television.

• Are you especially fond of any particular family show on television? What is it?

• There have been shows depicting families other than the traditional ones with a mom, a dad and kids. *The Andy Griffith Show* was one example. Name some others.

Family Ties

1. In the book that Christina Crawford wrote about her mother Joan, she claimed her mother lacked loving maternal instincts. Faye Dunaway starred in the movie version of the book. What was the title?

2. A nun, who was not a biological mother, spent her life serving the poor and the sick in Calcutta. She won the Nobel Peace Prize for her work. Her name is often used as a synonym for good. Who was she?

3. The third Sunday of June is officially designated to honor whom?

4. A famous artist painted his mother in a straight-backed chair, wearing a long black dress, a white lace cap, lace cuffs and she is holding a lace kerchief. Name the painting.

5. John Adams and John Quincy Adams were the second and sixth presidents of the United States. Name another father and son who have reached the highest office.

6. What was the relationship between Boston Mayor John F. "Honey-Fitz" Fitzgerald and a United States president?

7. Spencer Tracy starred with Elizabeth Taylor in the title role of a 1950 movie. Steve Martin played the role again in 1991. Their place in the family is mentioned in the film's title. What is it?

8. In 1907 Anna M. Jarvis started a campaign to strengthen family bonds by establishing a national day of recognition for a family member. What notable day is this?

9. Eddie Fisher used the words good and wonderful to describe somebody he missed very much. Who was it?

10. In Wadsworth's poem *Song of Hiawatha* what was Hiawatha's relationship to Nokomis?

11. When the *USS Juneau* went down, one family tragically lost five sons, which prompted the U.S. Navy to change its policy

for allowing brothers to serve on the same ship. Who were these brothers?

12. How are Theodore Roosevelt and Franklin D. Roosevelt related?

Answers on pages 117–118

Let's Talk

- There is an expression "blood is thicker than water." Do you believe this to be true? Why?

- Can you tell about an event in your own life where a family tie has made a strong impact?

- Of all the family relationships you have had, is there one person to whom you feel especially close? What makes that so?

Famous Doctors

1. What is the name of Robert Louis Stevenson's character who was the good personality opposite Mr. Hyde?

2. Name the famous doctor who performed the first heart transplant operation.

3. What was the name of the actor who played Dr. Galen Adams, the grumpy, lovable doctor on *Gunsmoke?*

4. Vince Edwards played a television neurosurgeon at County General Hospital. What was his character's name?

5. Who was Ben Casey's wild-haired boss, played by Sam Jaffe?

6. The doctor who developed the vaccine for polio was also a dedicated promoter of world peace. Who was he?

7. Rex Harrison played an eccentric, animal-loving English doctor in a 1967 movie. What doctor did he play?

8. Richard Chamberlain played a handsome, hard-working doctor at Blair General Hospital. What was the doctor's name?

9. Every good doctor needs an assistant. Dr. Marcus Welby had one who rode a motorcycle. Who played his assistant Dr. Steven Kiley?

10. A soft drink that is not necessarily prescribed for medical purposes sounds as though it could have been. What is it?

11. Theodor Geisel wrote numerous beloved children's books. What name did he use as the author?

12. Dr. Joe Gannon was the lead doctor in the television series *Medical Center.* Who played the role?

Answers on page 118

Let's Talk

• Donna Reed starred in *The Donna Reed Show*, and her character was married to Dr. Alex Stone. Why do you think she was considered a perfect homemaker and a model wife and mother?

• Not all doctors are lovable. Mary Shelley wrote a novel about one who has since become synonymous with horror. He was Dr. Victor Frankenstein. Discuss some of your experiences with *Frankenstein* movies or Halloween parties.

• Think back to a doctor you knew when you were very young. Discuss how his or her practice was different from your doctor's today. Did you like the earlier arrangement better? Why?

Famous Ships

1. A luxury liner owned by the White Star Lines met with disaster on April 15, 1912. Can you name this famous ship?

2. On September 2, 1945, General McArthur and Admirals Nimitz and Halsey accepted Japan's official surrender to the United States, ending World War II. This took place in Toyko Bay aboard what U.S. warship?

3. PT-109 was the boat commanded by what naval lieutenant who would later become a U.S. president?

4. A Gordon Lightfoot song immortalized 29 men who lost their lives when their ship went down in a storm on Lake Superior. What was the ship?

5. In literature, Ishmael was the lone survivor of the wreck of his ship, *The Pequod.* What was the name of the novel?

6. A group of settlers left England by sea in 1620 to establish a better life for themselves in the New World. On what ship did they sail?

7. Captain Hook is an important character in the story of *Peter Pan.* What ship did he command?

8. A prisoner aboard the British ship *The Minden* wrote "The Star Spangled Banner" while gazing at the shore at dawn. Who was he?

9. The king and queen of Spain issued three ships to Christopher Columbus in 1492. They were the *Niña,* the *Pinta* and the…

10. What is the name of the sunken battleship which lies in the waters off Hawaii, and is dedicated as a memorial to the Americans who lost their lives there?

11. What famous ship did the traitor Benedict Arnold use for his escape to England during the American Revolution?

12. Blackbeard was a famous pirate who terrorized the Atlantic until his ship sank in 1718. What was the name of his ship?

Answers on page 118

Let's Talk

• Sailing stories have long captured people's imaginations. Do you have a favorite sea story?

• Did any person here ever serve aboard a ship as a sailor? Tell of the experience.

• Have you owned a private boat that you enjoyed sailing, or have you ever taken a cruise that you would like to talk about?

Finish the Slogan

1. "Ace, the helpful…"

2. "You're in good hands with…"

3. AT&T says: "Reach Out and Touch..."

4. "See the USA in your..."

5. Lay's potato chips invites you to try this challenge: "Bet you can't eat..."

6. Hawaiian Punch says: "How about a nice..."

7. "How do you spell relief?"

8. Almond Joy says: "Sometimes you feel like a nut,..."

9. Hallmark says: "When you care enough to send..."

10. 1-800-Collect says: "Save a..."

11. "My bologna has a first name, it's... My bologna has a second name, it's..."

12. "Heinz, 57..."

   Answers on page 118

Let's Talk

• Most advertising slogans are set to music. Why?

• Are you more inclined to buy a product because the slogan sticks in your mind? Do you think that a lot of advertising makes the product better?

• Look around the room. Find an object and make up an advertising slogan to sell it. No, you don't need to set it to music!

Finish the Slogan Bonus Questions

1. "It's the quicker..." (Bounty)

2. "A little dab'll..." (Brylcreem)

3. "It tastes so good, cats ask for it..." (Meow Mix)

4. "Raise your hand if you're..."

5. "I love..."

6. "It's everywhere you..." (Visa)

7. "The breakfast of…"

8. "It's Miller…"

9. "Please don't squeeze the…"

10. "Because I'm…" (L'Oreal)

11. "Stick…" (T-Mobile)

12. "This… for you."

Answers on page 118

Fire and Heat

1. Sometimes wild fires are fought with something warmer than water. What is it?

2. When weather is exceptionally warm for a prolonged period of time, it is called a what?

3. The great fire of Chicago that started on October 8, 1871, is believed to have been caused when a cow kicked something. What was it?

4. A luminescent beetle that flies at night is called a what?

5. We all know that the big hunk Elvis Presley sizzled when his lover brightened his morning sky. What did he say that she used to light it?

6. You don't want to get close to what the Bible refers to as fire and brimstone. What is brimstone?

7. When lightning flashes out on the horizon in hot weather, but there is no thunder, what it is called?

8. On March 25, 1911, a fire killed 145 factory workers in New York City. Investigations resulted in laws to improve working conditions for laborers. What was that company's name?

9. The temperature at which fuel can ignite is called what?

10. Retreating Confederate soldiers set fire to several warehouses to prevent the Northern army from seizing their contents. What city was subsequently destroyed in the fire?

11. A pot of fire burns continually on the gravesite of President John F. Kennedy. What is it called?

12. Jose Feliciano must have been feeling chilly when he asked someone to give him a little warmth. What was his hit song?

Answers on page 118

Let's Talk

- Name ways people use fire in their everyday lives.

- The power of nature is evident during a storm when we see lightning. Did lightning ever strike near enough to you to frighten you? When was that?

- Certain foods don't taste good unless they're hot. Name some of them.

Firsts

1. What First Lady took such a keen interest in labor reform that she went down into a coal mine to inspect working conditions?

2. "Steamboat Willie" was Disney's first version of a cartoon personality that would eventually become a world-famous character. Who was this cheerful character?

3. Who was the first man to invent an aqualung that allowed divers to move underwater without air hoses?

4. Who was the first black man to play major league baseball?

5. Who was the first man to fly faster than the speed of sound?

6. What band leader/trombonist received the first gold record for selling a million records? The song was *Chattanooga Choo-Choo*.

7. Who was the first American reporter to go right to where the action was happening to televise news reports?

8. What comedienne was the first woman to deal with pregnancy on her television show?

9. Who was the first baseball player to achieve a lifetime total of 714 home run hits?

10. President Harry S. Truman was given the very first membership card in a national social program. What program was it?

11. Name the first U.S. President to resign this country's highest office.

12. Who was the first person to be given credit for inventing the motion picture camera?

Answers on pages 118–119

Let's Talk

• There have been more "firsts" during our lifetimes than at any time in history. Name as many firsts as you can.

• Starting with your birth, there have been countless firsts for you alone. Begin with your earliest memory and name some firsts.

• Baseball has a "first base." Football has "first downs." What other firsts are there in sports or our culture?

Foreign Language Hits

1. Los Lobos performed the soundtrack for a movie about the tragically short life of singer Ritchie Valens. Their Spanish language hit song was also the title of the film. What was it?

2. Peggy Lee thought she might "wait a day or two" for the rain to go away, but her playful record stayed ten weeks at the top in 1948. What was the title?

3. Vera Lynn's German language song about lovers being apart and hoping to be together again was in the top five in 1952. We still hear it on oldies stations. What was it?

4. Les Paul and Mary Ford asked for God's protection while they were apart in this song with a Spanish-language title. What was it?

5. Julius LaRosa said "she was so naughty" in Italian, and did some serious scat singing too, in his huge hit. Dean Martin also made his version of the same song. What was it?

6. Eartha Kitt purred like a kitten in her 1953 French-language song. When it reached the top, she knew for sure that, "It's Good." What was it?

7. Doris Day's 1956 hit song won the Oscar for Best Original Song in a movie. The title was foreign but her lyrics were English. What was it?

8. In 1958, Domenico Modungo made everybody feel blue as he sang in Italian. Dean Martin did his version of this one too, also in—what else—Italian! What was it?

9. Marlon Brando played a Korean War fighter pilot in love with a Japanese girl in a 1957 movie adaptation of a Mitchener novel. Red Buttons won Best Supporting Actor Oscar for his part. Name the movie.

10. This Israeli folk song, written more than 100 years ago, is still popular today and is traditionally played at Jewish weddings.

11. A folk song that was originally sung in French is a popular campfire and sing-along song. It asks the question "Are you sleeping?" Name it.

12. Kyu Sakamoto's hit song was not about food, but you might want to go out and order a Japanese meal after hearing it. What was it?

Answers on page 119

Let's Talk

- How many here were lucky enough to grow up in a home that spoke more than one language? Has knowing two languages benefited you during your life?

- We mentioned several songs and movies with foreign language phrases in them. Would these have been as appealing to you if they were strictly in English? Why?

- Did you or someone close to you come to this country knowing no English at all? Was it a difficult transition? Why?

Forgetting and Remembering

1. There is a little blue or white flower whose name says, "Don't fail to remember me." What is its common name?

2. The American fleet was attacked by the Japanese on December 7, 1941 in Hawaii. Do you remember the slogan (and song hit for Sammy Kaye) that resulted from that incident?

3. Two hundred sixty men died when a U.S. battleship was sunk in Havana harbor, resulting in the Spanish-American War. What slogan resulted?

4. In 1836, an outnumbered group of Texans fought Santa Anna's army at a little mission in San Antonio. Their heroic deaths became the battle cry that helped defeat the Mexicans six weeks later. What was it?

5. Abraham Lincoln said, "The world will little note nor long remember what we say here, but it can never forget what they did here." On what occasion did he say it?

6. One of the Ten Commandments tells us to remember something special and keep it holy. What is it?

7. There is an old saying that goes, "Women and (a certain animal) never forget an injury." What is that animal?

8. Groucho Marx once said, "I never forget a face, but in your case I'll... do what?

9. If a person acts in an unselfish way, or does something he would not normally do, we say he has done what to himself?

10. Another way to say you will reward someone with a gift or an honor, is to say you will do what?

11. A George M. Cohan song says "Remember me to Herald Square. Tell all the gang at Forty-second Street that I will soon be there." What is the song?

12. A song asks that you remember a place as well as "the cowboy who loved you so true." What is the place?

Answers on page 119

Let's Talk

- What is your very first memory? How old were you? Was it a trivial incident or was it something really important to your life?

- Sometimes an anxious moment will cause a person to forget something important, but then remember it later. Did that ever happen to you? What happened?

- Did you ever bump into a casual acquaintance and want to introduce him? His name was on the tip of your tongue, but you just couldn't remember it. How did you handle that embarrassing moment?

Green

1. Staff Sergeant Barry Sadler wrote and recorded a song to pay tribute to a cetain elite group of our fighting men. It became the top-selling single of 1966 and stayed at #1 for five weeks. Name it.

2. The color green is between which two colors in the rainbow?

3. If you see "an eyeball peepin' through a smoky cloud," what are you standing in front of?

4. The Brothers Four sang a lovely ballad about a place where rivers used to run. Where was it?

5. O. C. Smith told us there was "no such thing as Doctor Seuss, Disneyland and Mother Goose, no nursery rhymes." What song was he singing?

6. What is the green pigment in plants called that is essential to photosynthesis?

7. Ralph Nader ran for President of the United States in 2000 as candidate for which party?

8. The song about a condemned prisoner's longing to go back to his hometown and see his Mama, his Papa and Mary. What was it?

9. What is the self-governing island that is part of the Kingdom of Denmark, located to the Northeast of North America?

10. What is a slang name for jealousy?

11. "But by our next meeting, I'll hope to prove true" is a line from this popular children's sing-along song. What is it?

12. What is the name given to gases created by man's mishandling of the earth's resources?

Answers on page 119

Let's Talk

• Green is said to be a "relaxing" color for rooms. Do you feel particularly at ease when in a green room? Have you preferred it as a color for your walls at home?

• People use green dye in cake frostings. Why don't they use it in gravy and meat sauce?

• Yellow, red, brown, black, and white pets are common. Have you ever known anybody to own a green pet? If so, what was it?

Hair-Hair

1. A man's hair style with the hair clipped close to the head.

2. A description given to Elvis' hair because it was combed high off the forehead.

3. A word for having lots of hair.

4. Another word for hairpiece.

5. A handgun altered to fire with extreme ease is said to have what?

6. Cats are always coughing them up.

7. A name given to the style of your hair.

8. A beautician.

9. One who cuts a man's hair.

10. Scary or frightening.

11. No room to spare.

12. Insistence on trivial details.

Answers on page 119

Let's Talk

- Name as many hair styles as you can. (Hint: The Lady Di, Poodle cut, Pageboy)

- Name as many words as you can to describe hair.

- Some hair is so distinctive it is the first thing that comes to mind when you mention a certain person. Name some of those people. (Don King, the boxing promoter, is one example.)

Head Wear

1. What is the tall, cone-shaped head wear that once was put onto the head of someone who was perceived to be dimwitted?

2. Ladies used to buy head wear for a springtime religious observance. What did they call it?

3. Men in the Western part of the United States have a head wear that is so big they call it by a measuring container. What is it?

4. What is the name of the cloth that nuns wrap around the head and neck, leaving only their faces exposed?

5. What is a close fitting athletic hat with a bill, usually having a piece of elastic in back to adjust the size?

6. Name the protective head wear that is sometimes made of steel, and is worn by soldiers.

7. A stiff felt hat that has a round crown and a small curved brim is sometimes called a bowler. What is another name for it?

8. What is the name of the round Scottish cap that is flat on top and usually has a decorative pompom?

9. A stiff piece that is attached to the front of a hat or cap for use as a protective shield is called what?

10. One type of head wear is often made of gold and encrusted with precious jewels. It is worn by royalty. What is it called?

11. A knitted hat that can stretch over the ears for warmth can be long or short. Sometimes a tassel closes one end of it. What is it called?

12. A soft flat French hat that is pulled slightly forward on one side of the head is called what?

Answers on page 119

Let's Talk

- Until the last few years, people usually wore hats when they dressed up. Did you always wear a hat to church or dress up occasions? Do you wear one now?

- At one time, people wore nightcaps. Why would anybody wear one to bed?

- Hats may not be commonly worn accessories any more, but it makes sense to wear them for practical reasons. What type of hats do people wear as a matter of course today for protection?

Hills and Mountains

1. It's still a thrill to hear Fats Domino sing, "Though we're apart, you're part of me still." What hill was he talking about?

2. Name the campfire song in which "she'll be driving six white horses."

3. Patti Page sang that "you're welcome as the flowers" on a certain hill. Where was it?

4. An extinct volcanic cone in Japan is considered to be the sacred dwelling place of the gods. What is the name of this mountain?

5. One snow-covered mountain inspired a popular campfire song. Several kids' versions changed the words to, "On top of spaghetti." What is the mountain?

6. The mountain that sits on the Swiss-Italian border rises approximately 14,700 feet above sea level. What is this famous mountain in the Alps?

7. John Denver enjoyed the serenity of a clear blue mountain lake on a certain mountain range. What was the name of his tribute to the mountains he loved?

8. Earl Hamner, Jr. wrote a book about growing up with his large family on a mountain. Henry Fonda starred in a movie version. What was the book?

9. What is the mountain range in the Eastern United States that includes The White, The Green, Catskill, Allegheny, Blue Ridge, and Great Smoky Mountains?

10. What is the world's highest mountain?

11. General G. A. Custer lost a famous fight against the Sioux in a battleground nestled beneath what mountain range?

12. One of the most important battles of the Civil War took place on a little rounded hill outside of Gettysburg. Name the mountain.

Answers on pages 119–120

Let's Talk

- Did anybody here grow up in a mountainous region? Was your home rural or were you part of a large community? Tell about it.

- People often go on vacations to camp in the mountains. What is the attraction?

- Name some mountain activities that people enjoy. Are these some of your favorite things to do? Why?

Hollywood Hunks

1. What Hollywood hunk starred in and directed the shocker about a radio D.J. being stalked by a demented fan who insisted that he "Play 'Misty'" for her?

2. *The Sting* featured two of Hollywood's hunkiest hunks, one with gorgeous blue eyes and the other with a shock of blonde hair across his forehead. Who were these two guys?

3. Katharine Hepburn's real-life niece starred in a movie with her. The girl brought home a handsome man, and the big question was, *Guess Who's Coming To Dinner?* Who was the man?

4. What hunk has a name shared by a car manufacturer, and has played an archeologist with a name shared by a state?

5. What Hollywood hunk played just about everything, including a one-eyed drunken sheriff, a singing cowboy, a soldier, a sailor, a pilot, a cop, a Green Beret, a Roman centurion, and even Genghis Khan?

6. Name the gun-loving hunk who didn't use a gun in his all-time biggest hit movie. Instead, he destroyed Pharaoh's army by parting the Red Sea.

7. An Olympic champ went from swimming laps to swinging from trees with a chimp, and made a career of speaking in two- or three-word sentences. Who was he?

8. This hunk with a super body soared high in movies before suffering a devastating personal injury. He became a powerful spokesman for spinal cord research. Who was he?

9. One hunk played a memorable role of a sheriff married to a beautiful blonde Quaker girl. The bad guys were coming for him at twelve o'clock sharp, forcing him to choose between love and duty. Who was he?

10. The ladies got all lathered up by a Hollywood hunk in the 1975 movie *Shampoo,* and numerous Hollywood beauties couldn't wait to run their fingers through his hair. Who was he?

11. This movie hunk was a rebel without a cause in his real life. Though he died in his sports car at age 24, his pensive brooding is a trait that still personifies restless youth. Who was he?

12. One of Hitchcock's most exciting movie scenes took place on the treacherous face of Mount Rushmore. What movie hunk led Eva Marie Saint across this dangerous location?

Answers on page 120

Let's Talk

- We have named only a few Hollywood Hunks in this quiz. Who is your all-time favorite male actor? Why?

- Some extremely successful actors don't have classically handsome features. Two of them are Ernest Borgnine and Humphrey Bogart. Name a few others whose talent, not their profiles, carried them in their careers.

- Being multitalented never hurt anybody. Gene Kelly was also a successful director as well as dancer and actor. Frank Sinatra was a successful actor as well as singer. Actor Ronald Reagan even became president! Name other actors who can do more than just act.

Horses

1. Roy Rogers rode a beautiful golden palomino stallion in his movies. What was the horse's name?

2. Black Jack was the horse without a rider that carried a pair of boots pointing backward at the funeral of what famous man?

3. What famous person rode Brown Beauty during a midnight ride when he warned colonists that the British were coming?

4. George "Gabby" Hayes rode a horse with the name as cozy as a cotton comforter. What was the horse's name?

5. When one famous Western actor "got back in the saddle again," he always rode Champion. Who was the cowboy?

6. A team of eight horses is famous for representing the Budweiser Beer Company in commercials. What is this breed of horse?

7. Audrey Hepburn, playing Eliza Doolittle, lost her ladylike demeanor when she screamed for Dover to win at what famous English racetrack?

8. We affectionately called John Wayne "The Duke." What was the name of his horse in several movies?

9. War, Famine, Pestilence and Death are the names of what riders?

10. Ben Cartwright and his sons came riding in on their horses every week in *Bonanza*. What was Ben's horse's name?

11. Velvet Brown owned a horse that she rode to victory in *National Velvet*. What was her horse's name?

12. From which side does a rider mount his horse?

Answers on page 120

Let's Talk

- Have you ever ridden a horse? Did you ride often?

- Name some uses people have found for horses over the centuries.

- Could the American West have been won without the aid of horses? Why?

House Sweet Home

1. People who live in these houses should not throw stones.

2. The U.S. president lives in a large house with a simple name. What is it?

3. A building where the county government offices are located.

4. A building where female members of a college social organization live.

5. A 1978 movie that was a parody of college fraternity life and starred John Belushi.

6. A luxury dwelling on the top floor of a building.

7. An apartment building where the units are owned privately.

8. A home that shares a wall with another home is a…

9. This house is designed not for people but for the storage of goods or merchandise.

10. Hank Williams described the kind of house he moved into in his song *Move It On Over*. What kind of house was it?

11. A dome-shaped house made of blocks of snow or ice.

12. What is made of canvas, other fabric, or skins stretched over a frame and fastened to the ground by pegs?

Answers on page 120

Let's Talk

- Tell about some of the kinds of houses you have lived in.

- Some houses have remained in one family for generations. Did anybody here have a house with that kind of history? Discuss it.

- Many people are not building exceptionally large homes today. What are some reasons for that?

Initials

1. What do the initials M*A*S*H stand for in the movie and TV show of that same name?

2. What do the initials MGM stand for?

3. BC represents a way to denote years. What do these initials stand for?

4. BC also represents a place. Where is it?

5. What do the initials UK stand for?

6. "M" is the Roman numeral for what number?

7. L A can be the abbreviation for a city or a state. Name one or both.

8. You probably wouldn't want to come under the scrutiny of the CIA. What is it?

9. If you had kids, you may have been a member of the PTA What do the initials stand for?

10. What do the initials IQ stand for?

11. You might be nervous if you just received a letter from the FBI. What does that stand for?

12. We all know that a.m. means *ante meridiem*. What part of the day is this?

Answers on page 120

Let's Talk

- Name as many initials as you can that identify sports organizations.

- Name as many news organizations as you can that use initials for their names.

- Try to think of all the times you have used initials for things since you woke up this a.m. Tell the group what they are.

Instrumentally Speaking

1. What instrument has a slide to change the tones that it plays?

2. What is the piece of wood that attaches to a mouthpiece to produce sound?

3. Name the long slender musical instrument that is played by blowing across a hole near one end.

4. A six stringed instrument can be played with the fingers, and also with a pick. What is it?

5. This is a four- or five-stringed, circular bodied instrument that is essential to a Bluegrass band.

6. A musical instrument made by stretching skins across a frame.

7. A small drum with metal discs on its frame is played by shaking or striking with the fingers. What is this instrument?

8. A large, low-pitched brass instrument with a mouthpiece similar to that of a trumpet.

9. When blown, this primitive instrument creates a shrill sound.

10. Saxophones and clarinets are part of what family of instruments?

11. An instrument played by drawing a bow across a set of strings.

12. One of the Marx Brothers got his nickname because he was an accomplished musician. What did he play?

Answers on page 120

Let's Talk

- What is your favorite instrument? Do you have a favorite musician who plays it?

- Did you ever play an instrument? Do you still play? What is it?

- Here are a few suggestions on how to make simple, but fun, percussion instruments to use for keeping rhythm during sing-alongs: shake Ziploc bags with macaroni inside, roll up two magazines to strike together, or strike paper plates with metal spoons.

Islands

1. Harry Belafonte and James Mason dealt with labor problems on a West Indies island in a 1957 movie. They also had a few love problems with Joan Fontaine, Joan Collins, and Dorothy Dandridge. Name the movie.

2. What Hemingway book with an island in the title was made into a movie starring George C. Scott and Claire Bloom? It was about a sculptor and his three sons.

3. Kenny Rogers and Dolly Parton had a song with islands in the title, and it sailed away to become a big hit. Hint: The title came from a Hemingway book.

4. Name the island off the coast of San Francisco that was used as a federal prison.

5. What is the largest of the Hawaiian Islands?

6. Sicily is an island that lies in what sea?

7. Greenland is an island located between Iceland and what other large country?

8. Which continent is an island?

9. What island near New York City is 118 miles long and is between 12 and 20 miles wide at its narrowest and widest points?

10. What island is 90 miles south of Florida and lies at the entrance to the Gulf of Mexico?

11. Catalina Island is off the coast of what state?

12. In 1945 the U.S. forces won a key battle in the Pacific and raised the stars and stripes on Mt. Suribachi on what island?

Answers on page 121

Let's Talk

•   Does the idea of living on an island appeal to you? If so, where would you like your island to be? If not, why not?

•   What does the quote "no man is an island" mean to you?

•   If you expected to be stranded on an island for a long period of time and could only take one personal item, what would you take? Why?

It's About Time

1. A tall, free-standing clock with a family name.

2. A small timepiece that is set on a band and worn on a part of the body.

3. A Bill Haley recording was featured in *Blackboard Jungle* in 1955, and he had everybody fast-dancing for twelve full hours. What was the song?

4. This particular timepiece will wake you in the morning by playing music for you.

5. What do we call a large tower clock that takes its name from the bells in the British Parliament in Westminster Palace, London?

6. Time is determined when the sun casts a shadow on an upright piece set into a disc. This may not be precise, but it looks nice in your garden.

7. Workers say they "punch" this clock when they record their arrivals and departures.

8. Clocks are set an hour ahead of standard time to begin what official time change?

9. A device used to inform a chef that food has cooked a certain length of time.

10. A timepiece that is often used in races and has a hand to indicate fractions of a second.

11. A old-fashioned timepiece that was usually attached to a chain or ribbon and carried in a tiny pants pocket.

12. Time is determined when sand drains through a narrow neck between two glass containers, in this time piece.

Answers on page 121

Let's Talk

• Our society depends on clocks for almost everything. Tell how many things in your day are determined by the clock.

• Some watches are modern, digital, battery-operated pieces. Some are old family heirloom jewelry pieces. Can you tell about any special clocks or watches in your family?

• Imagine that all the clocks in the world stopped operating. What would be some of the consequences?

It's Grand

1. Your parent's maternal parent is your...

2. A large piano, often played in concert halls is a...

3. A body of individuals chosen to determine whether there is enough evidence to proceed with a trial is what?

4. You just won all the tricks in a hand of bridge. What do you call that?

5. Majesty, greatness, splendor, magnificence all mean...

6. Your son's or daughter's offspring is your...

7. The Colorado River dug a deep, long gorge through solid rock. What is it called?

8. Your mother's or father's uncle is your...

9. A famous auto race still run today originated in Paris in 1894 and caught worldwide enthusiasm. What is it?

10. A mountain range in Wyoming.

11. One of the world's largest dams in Washington State that was built for flood control, power, and irrigation.

12. Name the organization that consisted of veterans of the Northern army after the Civil War.

Answers on page 121

Let's Talk

- George M. Cohan wrote "You're A Grand Old Flag." Some synonyms for "grand" are impressive, imposing, magnificent, ostentatious, and splendid. Ask the group members to repeat the title, substituting one of those words for "grand." Would the song have been quite as successful?

- Do the same thing with "It's A Grand Night For Singing." Then ask everybody to name something that they think is especially "grand" and tell why they think so.

- A slang expression for a thousand dollars is "a grand." Would a broker be likely to say that a stock on the market is worth "a grand"? Would your bookie be more likely to say that you own him "a grand" or a thousand dollars?

Jimmy

1. What Jimmy went from enjoying great power and living in a really rich house to being retired and helping others build houses for the unknown and the poor?

2. Jimmy is another name for this tool used by burglars for prying something open. What tool is it?

3. Who is the singer/songwriter who usually performs in beach shorts and a bright tropical shirt? His songs are mainly about the sea, combing the beach, and drinking in "Margaritaville."

4. What "singing brakeman" traveled the rails singing of trains, mountains, and trees? He was also known as the "Blue Yodeler."

5. What Pennsylvania native was a real-life soldier who fought in military battles, and was also beloved as an actor? He had a slight speech stammer and won an Oscar for his role in *The Philadelphia Story.*

6. What Jimmy was a regular columnist for *Newsday*, and once advocated New York City secession as the 51st state?

7. Who was a daredevil pilot, an amateur boxer, and the recipient of the Medal of Honor for a daring bombing raid against Japan during WWII?

8. A hit song that had Martha and the Vandellas pleading to find out when their Jimmy was coming back. Maybe he was with Sheena Easton, who also recorded the song. What was it?

9. One Jimmy has a large television evangelism empire that is based in Baton Rouge, Louisiana. Who is he?

10. When Robert F. Kennedy was chief counsel of the Senate Labor Rackets Committee, he publicly accused a Jimmy of corruption. What Jimmy was he after?

11. This Jimmy was a dandy tap dancer turned movie actor who played good guys as well as tough guys with dirty faces.

12. This vehicle's name makes it sound like somebody's little boy, but in truth it is an SUV made by GMC. What is it?

Answers on page 121

Let's Talk

• Why do you suppose President Carter preferred to be called by his nickname instead of his given name, James? Would you have had more respect for him if he had used James?

• The men in this quiz come from many walks of life. Do you know any stories to tell about any of them?

• Is there a James in this room? Is there a Jim or a Jimmy?

John and Jack

1. What John was a little kid when he raised his right hand in a salute that became one of history's most memorable photographs?

2. What John was the second president of the United States, and the father of the sixth president?

3. A toy that springs up when the top is released is called what?

4. What is another name for heavy footwear that reaches the knee?

5. What is a pocketknife called if it has a handle that the blade can fold into?

6. What is name of the guy who turns the world white on a cold morning?

7. What is another name for a large, long-eared, strong-legged hare?

8. A child's game played with balls and pronged metal pieces is named what?

9. What is the generic name given to an unknown male person in a legal document?

10. Nearly two centuries ago, John Chapman traveled the Ohio Valley planting fruit. What was his nickname?

11. He was strong and he drove steel on the railroad, but his determination to prove he was better than a machine was his undoing. Who was this John?

12. The John whose short term as president of the United States has often been compared to the legendary kingdom of Camelot.

Answers on page 121

Let's Talk

- There are so many Johns in history. One is John Brown, the abolitionist who led a raid on the federal arsenal at Harpers Ferry, Virginia. Does anybody remember the song about him? Name some other famous men named John and mention what they did.

- Are you a John, or was there a John in your family? Was he called John or Jack? Tell about him.

- Think of people whose name was John and substitute Jack for fun. For instance, The apostle John would be the apostle Jack, and the film star would become Jack Wayne. Would that seem right to you?

Let's Celebrate

1. What holiday is named for a Roman martyr priest, recognized as a day for lovers?

2. What holy month commemorates the first revelation of the Koran?

3. What holiday is celebrated on the Second Sunday in May?

4. The Jewish New Year is called what?

5. Name the Jewish Day of Atonement, observed by fasting and prayer.

6. When is the official observance of Labor Day?

7. When is the official observance of Memorial Day?

8. Midnight December 31 is the official beginning of what holiday?

9. Father's Day is officially observed on which Sunday in June?

10. The fourth Thursday in November is what holiday?

11. The third Monday in February is what holiday?

12. The third Monday in January is what holiday?

    Answers on page 121

Let's Talk

- What is your favorite holiday? Do you have a traditional celebration for it? Tell the group what you do.

- Many of our holidays are observed on a Monday to create a three-day weekend for workers. Would you prefer to have the official observance on the actual date of all holidays? Why?

- Some people travel long distances to celebrate holidays with their families. Have each member of the group tell the greatest distance a family member travels to celebrate holidays. How long have they done this?

Let's Sit Down

1. What is a baby's chair called that brings him up to table height?

2. If you have a chair with two curved runners under the legs, what do you have?

3. Name the chair designed to tip back into a position for resting.

4. Give the name for a long bench used in churches.

5. A hard chair that is long enough to seat more than one person is called what?

6. A baby's chair with a hole in the seat, used for training away from diapers is known as a…

7. What is a rolling chair that gives mobility to people?

8. A padded chair that seats two people who are fond of each other is aptly called a…

9. The chair used by royalty is called a…

10. There is a shocking kind of chair that nobody wants to sit in. Name it.

11. Your favorite chair in the entire house is known as your…

12. The person who calls a meeting to order is the…

   Answers on page 122

Let's Talk

- Do you have a favorite chair? Where is it and why do you like it?

- Some chairs come as part of a set. A dinner table needs a chair. A desk wouldn't be very useful without a chair. What other chairs can you think of that are part of a set?

- Some places have seats lined up in rows. Name as many of them as you can.

Lucky Sevens

1. What number is considered to be lucky?

2. Pride, Avarice, Wrath, Envy, Gluttony, Sloth, and Lust are said to be what?

3. Who were Bashful, Doc, Dopey, Grumpy, Happy, Sleepy, and Sneezy?

4. Bob Hope played the head of a family with seven children. What was this 1955 movie?

5. Which one of the Seven Seas is not listed here? Antarctic, Arctic, North Atlantic, South Atlantic, Indian, North Pacific.

6. There are said to be seven virtues. They are faith, hope, charity or love, fortitude, justice, prudence, and...

7. The Great Wall of China is considered to be one of the what?

8. A person must be missing for seven years to be declared what?

9. What was the name given by the press to the burglars caught breaking into the Democratic Campaign Headquarters in 1972?

10. Extremely happy people often refer to themselves as being in a place that has a seven as part of its name. What is it?

11. What ancient city is said to have been built on seven hills?

12. What Yankee baseball player wore number 7 from the time he came up from the minors until he retired?

Answers on page 122

Let's Talk

- Seven can be lucky in product names too. This product has no caffeine, no artificial flavors and no artificial color, but the thing that makes it so refreshing is a secret: *7-Up.*

- Superstitions can be fun if they aren't taken too seriously. Do you think seven is a lucky number? Why or why not? Do you have an unlucky number?

- Your team is the champion if it wins four out of seven games. The sport is baseball and the big event is the World Series. Do you have any memorable World Series stories?

Mae West Wit: Finish the Quote

1. "His mother should have thrown him away and kept..."

2. "I like two kinds of men, domestic and..."

3. "When I'm good , I'm very, very good. When I'm bad, I'm..."

4. "I've been rich and I've been poor, and believe me, rich is..."

5. "A man in the house is worth two..."

6. "I used to be snow white, but I..."

7. "When a girl goes wrong, men go..."

8. W. C. Fields and Mae West co-wrote a movie wherein this term of endearment was used: "My little..."

9. "A woman in love can't be reasonable — or she probably wouldn't be..."

10. "Diets don't interest me. The only carrots that interest me are the carats in a..."

11. "Don't marry a man to reform him. That's what..."

12. Everybody knows the answer to this quote. Go around the room and have every woman say it in a Mae West voice. "Come up and..."

Answers on page 122

Mae West Wit: Finish the Quote Bonus Questions

1. "Lawyers always say, keep a diary, and someday it'll..."

2. "Don't let a man put anything over on you except..."

3. "When it comes to finances, remember that there are no withholding taxes on the..."

4. "I believe that it's better to be looked over than it is to be..."

5. "It's not the men in my life, but the..."

6. "Marriage is a great institution, but I'm not ready for..."

7. "It ain't no sin if you crack a few laws now and then, just so long as you..."

8. "You can say what you like about long dresses, but they cover a..."

9. "There are no good girls gone wrong, just..."

10. "I see you're a man with ideals. I guess I better be going while you've..."

11. "Too much of a good thing is..."

12. "When it comes to choosing between two evils, I always like to pick the one..."

Answers on page 122

Let's Talk

- Mae West's remarks were probably more shocking in her day than they would be today. Why is that so?

- By today's standards, Mae's figure probably would be considered too heavy. Regardless, she had a wonderful self-image. When a woman accepts herself as she is, are others more likely to accept her?

- Can you think of any more quotes attributed to Mae West? What are they?

Money, Money, Money

1. In this hit movie about a little orphan girl and her grandfather, Bing Crosby sang a song that made him enough small change to add up to big bucks. What was the song and movie title?

2. A person offers to pay very little to share another's concerns. What is the common saying for it?

3. Whose picture is on the $50 bill?

4. Whose picture is on the $20 bill?

5. Whose picture is on the $1 bill?

6. If you had five coins bearing the profile of Abraham Lincoln, how much money would you have?

7. If you had two coins bearing the profile of Thomas Jefferson, how much money would you have?

8. What is a person called if he collects coins?

9. If your bank balance had a number plus six zeroes, would you be a millionaire or a billionaire?

10. Name the small area in New York City that is considered to be the financial capital of the United States.

11. What signals the official opening of the Stock Market each day?

12. In 1 Timothy in the Bible, it is said that "the love of money is the root of…"

Answers on page 122

Let's Talk

- People strive for many things in their lives. Would you rather have great love or great riches? Why?

- Explain the saying, "Money begets money."

- What did Dickens mean when he said, "Money and goods are certainly the best of references"?

Nicknames

1. This rock star, proud to be born in the USA, had a string of hits in the 1970s and 1980s that was so long and so consistent that people started calling him "The Boss." Who is he?

2. Clara Bow was known as what girl?

3. Rudolph Valentino was often called the original what?

4. Lon Chaney's many characters earned him what nickname?

5. What was John Wayne affectionately called?

6. "007" was the code name for what Ian Fleming character?

7. "The Yankee Clipper" was a nickname given to whom?

8. A nickname was given to a Japanese radio personality in WWII. Who was this woman whose goal was to demoralize American troops through propaganda?

9. Another nickname was given to a woman who was Rose's German counterpart. Who was she?

10. This baseball star sported two nicknames. Who was "The Bambino?"

11. "Mr. Television" was a nickname given to what 1950s TV personality?

12. Edward Teach was a pirate who terrorized the seas around the West Indies. What was his nickname?

Answers on page 122

Let's Talk

- Do you have a nickname? What is it? How did you get it?

- Not all nicknames are used affectionately. Can you think of some that are intended to be hurtful?

- Some families have pet nicknames for their own members but the names are never used outside the family. Did anybody in your family have such a name?

Not People

1. *National Velvet* was a movie starring Elizabeth Taylor and Mickey Rooney. It was drama involving a young girl's beloved pet. What was the animal?

2. Lon Chaney, Jr. and Burgess Meredith played in the original movie version of a Steinbeck book. It was remade in 1981 with Robert Blake and Randy Quaid, and again in 1992 with John Malkovich and Gary Sinise. What was it?

3. Helen Reddy, Mickey Rooney, and Red Buttons made a Disney movie about a little orphan boy and his animated pet. What was the pet?

4. *Free Willie* was a movie about a delinquent boy who forms a friendship with an animal while working in an aquarium. What is the animal?

5. Beatrix Potter wrote many stories about small creatures. Her most famous character hopped all the way to lasting fame. Who was he?

6. In 1964 Peter Sellers played a bumbling detective, Inspector Clouseau. The movie was so popular that several sequels were made. What was it?

7. Disney brought many memorable characters to life, but one little boy wasn't a good liar because it always showed in his face. Who was he?

8. *Stuart Little* was a movie starring Geena Davis, who had a very unusual son. What was he?

9. *Bambi* was one of Disney's most beautiful movies. It was about a creature whose life cycles are said to parallel the seasons. What is the animal?

10. Peter, Paul and Mary's recording about an enchanted animal is now a classic, in spite of speculation about whether it promotes marijuana smoking. What is the song?

11. Elvis Presley may have been a little confused. All he wanted to be was the kind of toy a girl could cuddle. What did he just want to be?

12. The Irish Rovers song said that Noah's Ark drifted away without a certain creature aboard. What was it?

    Answers on page 123

Let's Talk

- Some of the first toys we give to babies are stuffed animals. Why do babies like them?

- Even adults enjoy letting their imaginations run free enough to accept movies about talking animals. Why is this true?

- Have you ever been especially fond of a character in a movie or book that was not human and not a real animal? What was that character?

Old Sayings, Part One

1. The squeaky wheel gets…

2. It's better to make a weak man your enemy than…

3. Fool me once, shame on you. Fool me twice…

4. Hell hath no fury like a woman…

5. If you want to dance, you have to…

6. A fool and his money are…

7. If you have to ask what it costs, you…

8. Today is the first day of…

9. Lie down with dogs and you will get…

10. Give me liberty or…

11. Old soldiers never die, they just…

12. Fools' names, like fools' faces, are often seen in…

    Answers on page 123

Let's Talk

- What does it mean to say a squeaky wheel gets the grease? How does that apply to our lives today?

- Most of us don't lie down with dogs, so why would that saying become part of our language?

- It goes without saying that today is the first day of the rest of our lives. So what?

Old Sayings, Part Two

1. If you give the devil a ride, he always wants…

2. A broken clock is right…

3. When you say "I can't" you are really saying…

4. If something sounds too good to be true, it…

5. A leopard can't change his…

6. Anyone can steer the ship when the sea is…

7. Be careful what you wish for—you just…

8. A person who has never made a mistake has never…

9. An ounce of prevention is worth…

10. It's easier to let the cat out of the bag than to…

11. If you see someone without a smile, give…

12. It's best to remain silent and thought a fool than to open your mouth and remove…

   Answers on page 123

Old Sayings, Part Three

1. Know which side your bread is…

2. Man may work from sun to sun but a woman's work is…

3. If you want to dance, you have to pay…

4. Play the hand you're...

5. It's better to have tried and failed than...

6. That's the way the cookie...

7. Don't fire until you see the...

8. Beware of Greeks bearing...

9. Cream rises to the...

10. Water finds its own...

11. Discretion is the better part of...

12. Don't bite off more than you can...

Answers on page 123

Let's Talk

- You may not play cards, so why would anyone tell you to play the hand you're dealt? What would be some consequences of ignoring that saying?

- Unless you're in the dairy business, why would you care whether cream rises to the top?

- Explain what it means to tell someone to know which side his bread is buttered on. Give some examples of people who did not know the truth to that saying.

Old Sayings, Part Four

1. Rain before seven, stop before...

2. Happy is the bride that the sun...

3. Red sky at night...

4. A chain is only as strong as its...

5. A little knowledge is a...

6. Count your blessings, not your...

7. A little faith can move...

8. Sharper than a serpent's tooth is a...

9. Beauty is in the eye of...

10. It's foolish to close the barn door after the...

11. The grass is always greener on the...

12. Winners never quit, and quitters...

Answers on page 123

One Hundred

1. What is The Old Hundredth?

2. What fairy tale heroine slept one hundred years until she was awakened with a kiss?

3. Contestants on Groucho Marx's TV show *You Bet Your Life* won $100 for saying something. What was it?

4. Take a hundred dogs and add an extra one, and you will have part of the title of a popular Walt Disney movie. What was it?

5. Where did Winnie The Pooh live?

6. How many centuries does it take to make a millennium?

7. A person who lives to be 100 years old is called a...

8. If you went to the 100-year celebration of a city, you would be attending what?

9. How many pounds is a hundredweight?

10. What American statesman said, "When angry, count ten before you speak; if very angry, a hundred."

11. A common expression is: ". . . the first hundred years are the..."

12. *Time* published a list of the 100 people it considered to be the most influential during a certain century. What was it?

Answers on pages 123–124

Let's Talk

- *Time* considered Winston Churchill, Franklin Roosevelt, Ronald Reagan, Billy Graham, and John Kennedy to be among the 100 most influential people of the 20th century for obvious reasons. Why did they include Adolph Hitler in that respected group?

- Elvis Presley, The Beatles, and Walt Disney were also included in *Time's* 100 most influential. Why?

- Can you remember when 100 dollars was once considered fairly good pay for a week's work? Discuss that distant memory.

One Name Is Enough

1. This great escape artist was born in Hungary but his feats are still remembered around the world 100 years later.

2. Who is considered the "father of radio" for inventing a way to send and receive sound waves without wires?

3. What woman scientist did research in the treatment of cancer with the use of radium?

4. Who wrote *God Bless America* and *White Christmas*?

5. What American president told Congress, "The world must be made safe for democracy"?

6. What former slave developed more than three hundred products from the peanut plant?

7. Who is the comic genius of silent films known as the little tramp?

8. What WWI American flying ace won the Medal of Honor for challenging seven enemy aircraft in an air battle and shooting down two of them?

9. What great soul of India spent his life advocating nonviolent change, then met a violent death?

10. Name the founder of psychoanalysis who introduced the "talking cure" to help people overcome their problems.

11. Which Roosevelt used the motto "Speak softly and carry a big stick?"

12. What inventor produced the first "horseless carriage?"

Answers on page 124

Let's Talk

- There are numerous people who have achieved such fame that they are known by one name alone. What others can you name?

- Great respect often accompanies great fame. If you met any of the people mentioned here, would you be formal and say "Mister, Miss, Mrs., or Doctor," instead of by the one well-known name?

- Only one of the dozen people mentioned above is a woman. There are countless women we know by one name only. Name some of them.

Oscar Loves the Ladies

1. What actress won the Oscar for her role as a young widow who took her son and headed west to become a singer? She needed to earn a living, so she took a job at Mel's Diner instead.

2. Who won an Oscar costarring with Yul Brynner in a 1956 movie about an amnesiac woman trying to pass as the heir to the Russian throne?

3. *The Silence of the Lambs* was anything but gentle! But it won Best Picture, Best Actor, Best Actress, Best Director, and Best Adapted Screenplay in 1991. Name the lady who caught a psycho killer and an Oscar at the same time.

4. We adore her for her voice, her fashions, and her many romances, but Oscar loved her best in a 1987 movie. Name the lady who played a young widow who fell in love with her fiancé's younger brother.

5. Kathy Bates won the 1990 Oscar by playing a psychotic romance novel fan who makes an author's life as miserable as possible. Name the movie.

6. Putting up with Jack Nicholson's phobias won this actress an Oscar in 1997. Jack thought his life was *As Good As It Gets* when he won, too. Who was the actress?

7. Dustin Hoffman was with this seductress in *The Graduate* (1967), but five years earlier it was no miracle that she won the Oscar for playing Helen Keller's teacher and companion. Who was she?

8. The role of Daisy could drive some actresses to distraction, but it looked like an easy ride for this 1989 Oscar winner. Who was she?

9. New Zealand was the setting for *The Piano* (1993) and the Best Actress Oscar went to the star of the show. Who was she?

10. *Dead Man Walking* made a powerful case for eliminating the death penalty and its star was powerful enough to win the Oscar in 1995. Who was she?

11. *Erin Brockovich* was a single mom who unintentionally turned activist. Who played the title role and won an Oscar doing it?

12. Not all nurses behave like angels of mercy, as this Oscar winning actress proved in *One Flew Over the Cuckoo's Nest*. Who played Nurse Ratchett?

Answers on page 124

Let's Talk

- Of all the female Oscar winners, which one is your favorite? What part did she play? Why did you like her?

- Do you watch the Oscars show to see who wins, or to see the fashions? Is there one dress that you particularly remember?

- Winning an Oscar does not guarantee an actress will continue getting good roles. Which of your favorite actresses went on to continued success, and which did not?

Oscar's Songs

1. Bob Hope's theme song "Thanks for the Memory" came from his first big feature film. The song was an Oscar winner in what 1938 movie?

2. The song in Disney's film *Pocahontas* simply blew the judges away, so they awarded it Best Song. What was it?

3. Although the 1950 Alan Ladd movie *Captain Carey, U.S.A.* is not regarded as a classic, the featured Nat King Cole song certainly is. What was the Da Vinci-inspired song?

4. Barbara Streisand starred in the 1976 remake of *A Star Is Born*. She cowrote that movie's Oscar winning song with Paul Williams. What was it?

5. Audrey Hepburn lit up the silver screen as Holly Golightly in *Breakfast at Tiffany's*. What won the Oscar for best song?

6. *Holiday Inn* starred Bing Crosby but Irving Berlin wrote the Oscar-winning song that has since become a Christmas classic. What was it?

7. Just two years after singing the Oscar hit from *Holiday Inn*, Bing was in *Going My Way* and his song won again. What was it?

8. *The Poseidon Adventure* had the actors struggling to get out of an upside-down ship, but the Oscar winning song promised things would get better. What was it?

9. Watching Disney's film *Song of the South* makes a wonderful day. And the Oscar-winning song from that movie still provides plenty of sunshine. What was it?

10. The 1945 movie *State Fair* was such a memorable movie that it might as well have been made yesterday. What was the Oscar-winning song from that movie?

11. The 1977 movie *You Light Up My Life* could have faded into obscurity except for the song from it that still shines. What was that Oscar winner?

12. Louis Gossett, Jr. proved he was right up there where he belonged when he took an Oscar for his performance in *An Officer and*

a Gentleman. The song from that movie didn't do too badly either. What was the name of that Oscar winner?

Answers on page 124

Let's Talk

- Were there any Oscar-winning songs listed here that you did not recognize? Do you have a favorite Oscar winner?

- Because most of these songs have gone on to become classics, do any of them remind you of a special event in your life? What is it?

- When a song wins an Oscar for Best Movie Song of the Year, was it the song or the singer that made it special? Did you disagree with any of these selections? Why?

Our Funny Language

1. Bob Hope and a lot of other "Soldiers in Greasepaint" went to U.S. military bases all over the world to boost our troops' morale. What organization arranged these celebrity tours?

2. Some singers sing words that make no sense, or notes that sound like musical instruments. What kind of singing is this?

3. If a teenage boy in the 1930s and 1940s wanted to ask a girl to do a fast dance with him, he might suggest that they destroy the floor covering. What was it he asked her to do?

4. Girl singers in the 1930s, 1940s, and 1950s were referred to by a slang name that might suggest they sat on a perch and nibbled seeds. What were they called?

5. Ham is a pork product, yet a popular beef product that contains no pork uses a pork product in its name. What is it?

6. Nobody wants his car to get overheated, but one name for a really cool car might suggest that it actually boiled over. What was the nickname?

7. You carry something in your wallet that sounds like food, but you can't eat it. Yet, you can't get a meal without it. What is it?

8. Using your foot to break a bad habit.

9. Finish this line from Little Richard's "Tutti-Frutti": A-wop-bop-a-loo-bop-a-wop…

10. What is another name for fun?

11. President Martin Van Buren was sometimes known as Old Kinderhook, from his birthplace in New York. This lead to a common slang expression used the world over today. What is it?

12. The Net. Dot-com. Google. Yahoo. With what do you associate these terms?

Answers on page 124

Let's Talk

• Kids have always used slang words to express themselves. Why do they do this?

• Think back on your own teenage years. What were some of the slang words that your group used?

• The Internet has created a whole new language in the past few years. List as many of these new words as you can.

Patriotic Songs

1. What John Philip Sousa march proudly proclaims that the American flag will fly until the end of time?

2. Colonial soldiers turned what British drinking song into an inspiring battle song that personifies the American spirit to this day?

3. Julia Ward Howe wrote a poem that was set to the music of "John Brown's Body" and it became the fighting anthem of the Northern Army in the Civil War. What was the name of it?

4. James Cagney won an Oscar for playing George M. Cohan. He did his most memorable dance to a song that is also the name of the movie. What was it?

5. Kate Smith's most famous recording could easily be mistaken for a prayer. This classic song is synonymous with patriotism.

6. The very title of a song by George M. Cohan pays a great compliment to the symbol of our country. Name the song in which he speaks directly to our high-flying flag.

7. Rough terrain and dust can't keep our soldiers from shouting loud and strong as they march behind their mounted guns. What is the Army's song?

8. What was the rousing anthem that the Southern army marched to in the Civil war?

9. What march by Sr. Edward Elgar is traditionally played at graduations and occasions of honor?

10. One might wonder whether Sousa named this march after the military camp or the newspaper. What was it?

11. What patriotic song begins with a question?

12. Name the patriotic song that declares God has spread his grace over the entire country from one ocean to the other.

Answers on page 124

Let's Talk

• When a marching band plays patriotic songs, do you get a lump in your throat? Why or why not?

• Are there any veterans here? Do patriotic marches bring back memories of your time in the service? Tell us about it.

• Would a Fourth of July parade be complete without a marching band playing patriotic songs? Why?

Presidential Peculiarities

1. What piano-playing president was left-handed?

2. What is Jimmy Carter's middle name?

3. What president had a movie-star smile in spite of the fact that he loved eating jellybeans?

4. President James Garfield was one of our two presidents to be born in a log cabin. Name the other one.

5. Who was the only U.S. president to resign from that office?

6. One president was well-known as a horseman, and he was also the first president to ride in an automobile. Who was he?

7. Only one U.S. president was once engaged, but never married. With no official First Lady, he had his niece serve as official White House hostess. Can you name him?

8. Who was the only man to first serve as president of the United States then to serve as Chief Justice of the Supreme Court?

9. One president served two terms, but they were not consecutive. He is therefore listed officially as the 22nd and 24th president of the United States. Who was he?

10. What U.S. president survived two assassination attempts?

11. Three U.S. presidents remained childless all their lives: Madison, Polk, and Buchanan. What else did these commanders-in-chief have in common?

12. Who was the first U.S. president to be divorced?

Answers on pages 124–125

Let's Talk

- Today, the president's personal life is not as closely guarded as it once was. To what do you attribute this? Do you think we know too much about our public officials' personal lives? Why or why not?

- There have always been attempts on the president's life. Do you think the president is safer today than in previous years because of Secret Service protection?

- Harry Truman's piano playing and plain talking seemed to make him a "man of the people." What other presidents do you feel you could have liked as a person? Why?

Queens and Kings

1. The record *Dancing Queen* topped the world charts in 1977. The group who recorded it was Sweden's second-largest export. Who were they?

2. What legendary medieval king presided over a Round Table at Camelot?

3. Roger Miller traveled to the top of music charts with a record about a somewhat less than royal king wearing an old worn out suit and shoes. What was the name of the song?

4. Humphrey Bogart and Katharine Hepburn gave royal performances as a hard drinking riverboat captain and his prudish passenger as they fought dangers during World War I. Name the boat and the movie.

5. What British king gave up the British Throne for "the woman I love?"

6. Philip Mountbatten married what British queen?

7. Name the American girl who married a prince and gave up her position as one of the Queens of the Silver Screen.

8. *God Save The King (or Queen)* is the national anthem of what country?

9. What king kidnapped Ann Darrow and climbed up the side of the Empire State Building with her in his arms?

10. What king fought Bobby Riggs in "The Battle of the Sexes" and won?

11. A Cunard ocean liner with a royal name was retired and turned into a floating museum at a pier in Long Beach, California. What is the name of the ship?

12. The wildflower that is also known as a wild carrot has feathery foliage and a white lacy blossom. What is it?

Answers on page 125

Let's Talk

- Do you have a favorite historical king or a queen? Tell why that person has earned your respect—or not.

- Some scholars predict that the British Monarchy will become a thing of the past. Do you believe it should be eliminated? Why?

- Why do you think royal weddings capture people's imagination?

Red

1. Some people react to embarrassment by having a part of their body turn red. What body part is it?

2. What is the official tree of the State of California?

3. Hester Prynne wore a red letter embroidered on her dress. What letter was it?

4. The 40th wedding anniversary is celebrated by giving what red stone?

5. Glinda, the Good Witch of the North gave Dorothy a pair of what?

6. If you are in a railway station and want help with your luggage, you will look for what?

7. Evelyn "Billie" Frechette was called "The Lady in Red" by newspapers, because she was wearing a red dress when she was leaving a movie with what famous criminal when he was killed?

8. Bugs Bunny spent a lot of time tormenting Elmer J. Fudd. What did Elmer wear that were always red?

9. When red blood cell production is below normal, the resulting condition is called what?

10. A red wedding gown is traditionally worn by a bride in what country?

11. If you fought in the American Revolution and wore a uniform with a red coat, whose army would you be fighting for?

12. Would you consider your business to be doing well or failing if your books were found to be "in the red?"

    Answers on page 125

Let's Talk

- What does it mean to be "caught red-handed?"

- A person accused of being a "Red" is thought to be a member of the Communist party? Do you recall the mood of the country during the McCarthy hearings in the 1950s?

- What does the expression "roll out the red carpet" mean? Think of as many other expressions as possible that use the word "red."

Rock

1. A craze that swept the nation had people buying stones with little sayings written on them. What were they called?

2. When the Mayflower reached the new world, the Pilgrims stepped onto what rock?

3. The hand that rocks the cradle does what?

4. "When the bough breaks the cradle will fall" is a line from what nursery rhyme?

5. A marriage that has turned sour is said to be on what?

6. When rock and roll music was blended with hillbilly music, the new sound was called what?

7. What rock is proclaimed in song as being a girl's best friend?

8. Melted rock spewing from a hole in the earth is called what?

9. Name the rock that stands in a strait that connects the Atlantic Ocean with the Mediterranean Sea. Its name symbolizes strength.

10. If you ask for your drink to be "on the rocks," what are you asking to be included in it?

11. Bill Haley and His Comets promised they were going to do something to a time piece. What was it?

12. "The Rock" was a name given to a federal prison in San Francisco Bay. What was it?

Answers on page 125

Let's Talk

• Fairy tales often had a moral lesson. The Three Little Pigs built their houses of straw, twigs (or sticks) and bricks (or rock). What was the moral to this story?

• Has anybody ever referred to you as a rock? What did they mean? Were they right? Is that how you see yourself?

• Would Sylvester Stallone's "Rocky" movies have been as convincing if the hero's nickname had been "Les" or "Wimpy"? Discuss the power of a powerful name.

Saints Go Marching

1. You may not be saintly, but you'll want to go marching when you hear this song that has been played as Dixieland jazz, religious, sing-along, and any number of other styles.

2. A young 15th century girl said voices told her to lead the French army against the English. She led them and won, but she was burned for doing it. Who was she?

3. On what day each year do the swallows return to the Mission San Juan Capistrano?

4. Tom Sawyer and Huckleberry Finn grew up in a small town in Missouri. What was it?

5. Name the city in Russia that was designed by Peter the Great as a cultural and historical center.

6. St. Patrick is the patron saint of what country?

7. The patron saint of England is often shown slaying a dragon. What is his name?

8. Al Capone's men dressed up like policemen and machine-gunned seven members of a rival gangster mob in Chicago in 1929. What is this famous gang-murder called?

9. St. Croix and St. Thomas are two of the three U.S. held islands in what island group?

10. What is the third U.S. Virgin Island?

11. The Gateway Arch is the tallest monument in the United States and stands 630 feet. In what city is it located?

12. Speaking of St. Louis, name the song written by W. C. Handy in which he says he hates to see the evening sun go down.

Answers on page 125

Let's Talk

• Sometimes people referred to people they admire as "saints." Why is that?

• If you divided everybody you know into "saints" or "sinners," which side would have the most people on it? Why?

• The St. Louis hockey team is the only team named for a song. Can you name some of the artists who have recorded "The St. Louis Blues"?

Ships and Boats

1. Humphrey Bogart was a paranoid sea captain facing two dangerous foes (a typhoon and his own officers) in what movie?

2. A song recorded by Creedence Clearwater Revival is about a river boat. It burned its way to the top and has kept on turning since 1969. What was the boat's name?

3. The U.S. Navy names its battleships after what?

4. The Beach Boys and The Kingston Trio all took their grandfather with them on a boat, but they all still wanted to go home. What was the name of the boat?

5. Marlon Brando was a handsome young Fletcher Christian sailing the South Pacific. His costar Tarita, gave no revolt when she later married him. What was the film?

6. Jerome Kern and Oscar Hammerstein II wrote a musical about life on the Old Man River. What was the show's name?

7. U.S. Naval cruisers are named after what?

8. Naval destroyers are named after what?

9. U.S. Navy submarines were once primarily named after what?

10. Steve McQueen cruised the Yangtze River in a U.S. gunboat in an action/romance movie, which costarred Candice Bergen. What was the movie?

11. What is a Cajun style flat-bottomed, wooden boat? (Hint: Think about Hank Williams and a plate of jambalaya.)

12. Pitcairn Island is said to be inhabited by descendants of mutineers from what famous ship?

Answers on page 125

Let's Talk

• Bogart must have enjoyed boats, especially when he got sober enough to pilot Katharine Hepburn downriver in *The African Queen*. Discuss some of your favorite scenes.

• There has been much discussion in the past few years whether the *Titanic* should be raised. What is your opinion on the matter?

• Would you rather take a cruise down the Mississippi on a paddlewheeler or go to the Bahamas on a giant cruise liner? Why?

Shoes: What Kind?

1. Pat Boone

2. Elvis

3. Dorothy

4. The Netherlands

5. Flat sole that blends seamlessly into the heel

6. Flat shoe with a strap coming up between the first two toes

7. A sole with openwork straps

8. Native Americans

9. Sport shoe, usually made of canvas and rubber

10. Slang expression for being discharged from a job

11. Soft, knitted foot coverings for babies

12. Shoes worn by ballerinas

   Answers on page 126

Let's Talk

- If you could only own one pair of shoes, what would it be? Why?

- Do you remember the old-fashioned rubber overshoes you wore to school when you were a kid? What were some advantages it had over today's boots? What are some disadvantages?

- High-heeled shoes look dressy and glamorous. Discuss their advantages and disadvantages. Do you wear them today? What is the highest heel you or anybody close to you ever wore?

Shoes Bonus Questions

1. Cinderella lost her glass slipper when the clock struck...

2. Before shoestrings were introduced in shoemaking, shoes were commonly fastened with...

3. A shoelace goes through a tube to prevent its unraveling and to help push it through the eyelets. What is that tube called?

4. Policemen and detectives often preferred the soft comfort of rubber-soled shoes because they spent a lot of time on their feet. What derogatory nickname did that shoe earn them?

5. When rubber soles were first attached to canvas uppers, the result was a quiet shoe, which further resulted in the nickname of...

6. Loose-fitting shoes can be made a little more snug by inserting a pair of...

7. The god Mercury wore something on his heels. What were they?

8. The Lily Foot shoe was worn by Chinese women whose feet had been...

9. There was an old woman who lived in a shoe. What did she have?

10. Shoes with lifts hidden inside to add to a man's height are called...

11. A dressy man's shoe with pointed inset of leather at the toe is a...

12. Protective shoes worn in some workplaces are called...

Answers on page 126

Skin

1. We stress inner goodness by saying that one human quality is only as deep as the skin. What are we talking about?

2. What do we call a really close-fitting garment?

3. What is the name we give a person who is extremely miserly with his money?

4. People who swim down deep using no special equipment except flippers and oxygen masks are said to be doing what?

5. A person who removes the hides from animals is called a what?

6. A person who drives teams of mules is called a what?

7. What are very thin people often called?

8. The edible fruit of a banana is covered with a thick what?

9. Parchment is the skin of a goat or sheep that is used for writing in place of another substance. What does it replace?

10. Name the lizard that is capable of changing the color of its skin.

11. Who said, " I have a dream that my four little children will one day live in a nation where they will not be judged by the color of their skin, but by the content of their character"?

12. A certain animal may shed its skin seven times or more the first year of its life to allow for its body's growth. What animal is this?

Answers on page 126

Let's Talk

• A person who avoids a dangerous situation without harming himself is said to have escaped "by the skin of his teeth." We all know that teeth don't have skin, so why say that?

• Puppies and kittens have very loose skin. Why didn't nature make it fit better?

• Most animals have protective coverings over their skin. Mankind makes his own. What are some of the elements we are protecting against with our clothing?

Slogans and Mottos

1. The Hippie slogan during the Vietnam War: Make love…

2. Brylcreem says: A little dab'll…

3. Star-Kist Tuna's ad says: Charley, they don't want tunas with good taste, they want tunas that…

4. The King of Beers is…

5. The official motto of the Boy Scouts is…

6. President Franklin D. Roosevelt referred to December 7, 1941, as a date which will live in…

7. Whose motto is "We learn to do by doing?"

8. The journalist's slogan is: Who, What, Where, When and…

9. Maxwell House Coffee says it is good to the very…

10. What slogan appears on coins of the United States?

11. Complete this Packard slogan: Ask the man…

12. "Double your pleasure. Double your fun." With what?

Answers on page 126

Let's Talk

- Some of our slogans rhyme. Some don't. Name as many rhyming slogans as you can. Name a few that don't.

- Advertising companies try to create catchy slogans that will make us want to buy the products they are selling. Think of items in your medicine cabinet and on your dresser. Name the item and the slogan that goes with it.

- Look around the room. Have each person pick something and make up a one-line slogan for it.

Slogans and Mottos Bonus Questions

1. I'd walk a mile for a…

2. You've come a long way…

3. Doctors recommend…

4. Just what the doctor…

5. Not a… in a carload.

6. …tastes good, like a cigarette should.

7. Smoke a… to feel your level best.

8. …soothe your T-Zone.

9. More doctors smoke… than any other cigarette.

10. You're never alone with a…

11. Would a gentleman offer a lady a…

12. Chew… (This slogan was painted on the side of nearly every barn in the country.)

Answers on page 126

Stars

1. In 1953 Perry Como spent 39 weeks on the Hit Parade warning everybody against the dangers of letting the stars do something. What was it?

2. Depending on their position of their orbits, the planets Mercury and Venus are called the Morning Star or the what?

3. The surface of Mars contains a lot of iron dust. The color it creates gives Mars its nickname. What color is it?

4. The moon shines because the sun reflects off of something on its surface. What is it?

5. What is the brightest object in our night sky?

6. There is a fancy name for what we see stars doing. It is called stellar scintillation or astronomical scintillation. One simple word for what we see is…

7. Stars twinkle when they are observed through thick layers of something in motion. What is it?

8. Stars overhead seem to twinkle less than those near the horizon because their light must move through more air near the horizon. What is the moving and bending of a star's light called?

9. The earth depends on a ball of hot gas for heat. What is this star called?

10. What do we call a person who studies the heavenly bodies?

11. A movie with "star" in its title was made in 1937 starring Fredric March, again in 1954 with Judy Garland, and again in 1976 with Barbra Streisand. What was it?

12. A pale white, blotchy streak that we observe in the night sky is actually a band of countless stars. What is it called?

Answers on pages 126–127

Let's Talk

• "Starry Night" is a famous painting by Vincent Van Gogh. Is there a starry night memory in particular you can share?

- Does one starry night in particular stand out in your mind? Tell the group about it.

- When you look at the stars and realize the earth is just one bright dot in the heavens, can you consider the possibility of life on more than one planet? Why or why not?

Suns and Moons

1. The moon is not always the same distance from Earth. How can the distance change?

2. In 1974, Gordon Lightfoot gave a warning, "You'd better take care if I find you've been creeping round my back stair." What was this song?

3. That same year, John Denver reacted a little differently to the sun's rays, saying they made him happy, made him cry, and made him high. What was his song?

4. A man may work from sun to sun but a woman's work…

5. Greer Garson and Ralph Bellamy shine in a movie about Franklin and Eleanor Roosevelt in his battle against polio. What was this 1960 movie?

6. Gale Garnett said she didn't trust any man, but promised to take just one year to laugh every day. What was her 1960s hit song?

7. One of the first songs that children usually learn stays with them through their sing-along and campfire years. We can't take it away from them because it makes them happy.

8. The Apollo 11 mission first landed man on the moon in 1969. Who was the first man to set foot on the moon's surface?

9. A lunar eclipse happens when sunlight is blocked as the moon passes through what?

10. People used to think the moon was made of cheese because it appears yellow and its craters look like what?

11. George Burns and Walter Matthau portrayed two grumpy ex-vaudeville actors who teamed up for a TV special. What was the name of this 1975 Neil Simon movie?

12. What is the name given to an alcoholic beverage that is made under sneaky circumstances to avoid the payment of revenue?

Answers on page 127

Let's Talk

• The sun and the moon have always held man's imagination. Talk about some people who have worshipped the sun.

• Do you prefer to be outside in the daytime enjoying the sun, or at night so you can enjoy the moon? Why?

• Discuss how the sun affects us every day.

Tom and Thomas

1. This red headed Tom authored one of America's most important Declarations.

2. A man who likes to run around at night and see a variety of ladies has the nickname of what four legged Tom?

3. A gobbler whose mate is called a hen.

4. A war weapon used by the Algonquian Indians.

5. A nickname given to a young girl who would rather play with boys than dolls.

6. A fun-loving boy who was one of Mark Twain's most famous characters.

7. A cat and mouse team created by Hanna-Barbera and made famous in MGM cartoons.

8. A 32-inch tall dwarf who worked for P.T. Barnum went by the title of General. Who was he?

9. "It's not unusual" to still be hearing songs that a curly-haired Welshman has been singing since the 1960s. His female fans

respond to the sight of his unbuttoned shirt by throwing love notes and keys onto the stage. Who is he?

10. What Tom was governor of New York and made two unsuccessful runs for president on the Republican Party?

11. One of the Twelve Apostles, Thomas, did not believe the resurrection until he actually touched Jesus' side. His action has given a nickname to people who do not believe. What is it?

12. An animated cartoon character named Tom wore a funnel on his head. Who was he?

Answers on page 127

Let's Talk

• Is anybody here named Thomas? Was it a family name? Do you prefer the short form of Tom or even Tommy?

• General Tommy Franks served nearly four decades in the U.S. Army, earned three Purple Hearts for battle wounds and three Bronze Stars for valor. Do you remember his participation in the first Operation Desert Storm? Does the nickname "Tommy" seem appropriate for a soldier?

• Tomfoolery is another name for silly behavior or just plain nonsense. When you were a kid, you probably did plenty of it. Would you care to share some of your experiences with tomfoolery with the group?

Trains

1. What singing group would you expect to meet if you took "The Last Train to Clarksville"?

2. The Chesapeake and Ohio Railroad had an advertising slogan for their sleeper cars that promised you would sleep like a…

3. What song would you play on your banjo if you and your girlfriend Dinah took a railroad job just to pass the time away?

4. Judy Garland had everybody clanging and dinging what catchy song from her 1944 classic movie *Meet Me in St. Louis*?

5. The United States was changed forever on May 10, 1869, when the Union Pacific tracks were joined with those of the Central Pacific Railroad. At what town did this occur?

6. Ingrid Bergman won a Best Supporting Actress Oscar in 1974 for her role in the movie adaptation of Agatha Christie's novel that took place on a train. What was its title?

7. Burt Lancaster starred in a 1964 thriller about French art treasures being taken by train to Germany during World War II. What was the movie?

8. RCA Victor awarded Glenn Miller its first solid gold record for his recording about what train whose name sounded like a child's toy?

9. What is the name of a folk song that is believed to be based on the life of railroad man, John Luther Jones?

10. The Underground Railroad was not a railroad, but a route used by slaves escaping to Canada. Who was often called the "Moses of Her People" for using it to lead so many people to freedom?

11. What is the name given to a railroad car that was specially fit to allow passengers to sleep?

12. The last car on a freight train has a name. What is it?

Answers on page 127

Let's Talk

- Did you ever take a long rail trip? Where did you go? Tell about it.

- On your rail trip, did you have a meal in the elegant dining car with its white tablecloths and white uniformed waiters? What else can you tell about the experience?

- The opposite of elegance would be "riding the rails," a common practice during the Great Depression. What stories have you heard about men who sneaked aboard boxcars during that era?

Trees and Flowers

1. Jack Lemmon and Lee Remick were an alcoholic couple in what 1962 movie? (Hint: The Oscar winning title song was also the name of the movie.)

2. The Statler Brothers may have smoked cigarettes and played solitaire 'til dawn in the song, but they went very public when it became a top hit in 1966. What song is it?

3. Barbra Streisand and Neil Diamond sang sadly about losing their sense of togetherness, but they gave each other bouquets when their duet became a smash hit.

4. A 1958 Rodgers and Hammerstein musical that returned to Broadway in 2002, takes place on Grant Avenue, San Francisco, California, about a man from a traditional Chinese American family in love with a night club dancer. What is it?

5. The wood from what tree is traditionally used to make baseball bats because of its hardness?

6. Several varieties of trees, as well as straw, sugar cane, and hemp, are turned into pulp and made into what useful substance?

7. Fibers from the raffia palm tree are often used to make what?

8. What flower grows in the water and has leaves that float on the surface?

9. Some plants make beautiful flowers that can also produce dangerous substances. The drug heroin is derived from what flower?

10. The sap from some trees is collected and made into a sweet edible substance. What tree is it?

11. What type of tree is the world's tallest?

12. A flower differs from a weed because a weed is not…

Answers on page 127

Let's Talk

- Trees are useful for numerous reasons. Ask everybody in the room to name some of them.

- Flowers add color and beauty to every setting, inside and out. What is your favorite flower? Do you prefer a certain color? Do you like flowers for their beauty or their fragrance, or both?

- Ask everybody to tell a story involving a tree or a flower that was important in their life.

TV Characters

1. TV's *Howdy Doody Show* had a red-haired clown who used a horn instead of talking. What was his name?

2. *American Bandstand* was initially broadcast from Philadelphia. Who was the youthful host of the show?

3. Dr. Zorba was the wild-haired physician who played department head for what 1960s TV doctor?

4. 1970s TV Doctor Steven Kiley was assistant to which more famous TV doctor?

5. What actor played the desk clerk at the Empty Arms Hotel in the TV series *Hee Haw*?

6. Sesame Street's Bert has a special pal who was also his roommate. What is his name?

7. Captain Kangaroo had a good friend whose name was directly related to his choice of trousers. Who was he?

8. Shirley Jones was the mother of a family of singing children in what TV series?

9. In the TV show *Dragnet,* Officer Bill Gannon was a partner to what other officer?

10. In the series *Gunsmoke,* Milburn Stone played a frontier doctor. What was his name?

11. What was Ed McMahon's standard introduction at the beginning of every episode of *The Tonight Show*?

12. What singer had a regular Christmas show along with his regular show, from 1962–1967 that featured his singing brothers and his wife and children?

Answers on page 127

Let's Talk

- Did you enjoy the earlier television shows of the 1970s and 1980s? What was your favorite type (the variety shows, the family shows, the hospital dramas, or something else)?

- Television comedians like Johnny Carson in the 1970s, and Jay Leno and David Letterman today, can shape our cultural opinions on everything from politics to morals. Do they sway your opinions?

- Many television shows today have a heavy emphasis on violence. Do you think they have anything to do with the crime rate? Explain your position.

Twain-isms

1. Work consists of whatever a body is obliged to do—Play consists of whatever a body is...

2. When in doubt, tell...

3. Man is the only animal that blushes or...

4. When angry, count four; when very angry...

5. Familiarity breeds contempt—and...

6. As out of place as a Presbyterian...

7. Always do right. That will gratify some people, and...

8. Adam did not want the apple for the apple's sake, he wanted it only because...

9. Thunder is good, thunder is impressive; but it is lightning that does...

10. One of the most striking differences between a cat and a lie is that a cat...

11. A baby is an inestimable blessing and...

12. I was gratified to be able to answer promptly, and I did. I said...

Answers on pages 127–128

Let's Talk

- Mark Twain was born in 1835. He died nearly a century ago, in 1910. Why are his characters still so beloved today?

- Mark Twain is still quoted often. What is it about his observations that apply to today's world, when it has changed so much since his lifetime?

- Do you have a favorite Mark Twain story, or a favorite character that he created? Would you enjoy hearing one of his classics read aloud, chapter by chapter, over a period of time?

Twain-isms Bonus Questions

1. Be careful about reading health books. You may die of a...

2. Courage is resistance to fear, mastery of fear—not...

3. Don't go around saying the world owes you a living. The world owes you nothing. It was...

4. Honesty is the best policy—when there is...

5. I have been through some terrible things in my life, some of which...

6. I have never taken any exercise except sleeping and...

7. I have never let my schooling interfere with my...

8. It is better to deserve honors and not have them than to have them and...

9. It is curious that physical courage should be so common in the world and moral courage...

10. Let us be thankful for the fools. But for them the rest of us could not...

11. The human race has only one really effective weapon, and that is...

12. The worst loneliness is to not be comfortable with...

Answers on page 128

Walls

1. A wall that is said to be the ruin of a Biblical temple is still an important place in Jerusalem today. What is it?

2. President Ronald Reagan urged Soviet leader Mikhail Gorbachev to tear down a wall that had stood since the end of World War II. What wall was it?

3. An ancient wall is 1,500 miles long and dates from the Ming Dynasty (1368–1644). What wall is it?

4. On what black granite wall in Washington, D.C. are the names of 58,245 men and women etched?

5. Roman soldiers patrolled Hadrian's Wall to watch for Celtic raiders, as far back as 120 A.D. In what country will you find the remains of this wall?

6. What do you do when you make someone extremely tense?

7. What famous nursery rhyme character sat on a wall?

8. What general was said to be standing like a stone wall at the Battle of Bull Run?

9. Who was leading the children of Israel when the water parted and became a wall on their right and on their left?

10. When the stock market crashed in October of 1929, a headline announced that a certain street had laid an egg. What street?

11. What Biblical walls fell down when trumpets were blown?

12. Instead of trying to break through the walls of Troy by force, the ancient Greeks gave the city a unique gift. What was it?

Answers on page 128

Let's Talk

- Walls may have been effective in ancient times to keep invaders out of a city. Why would they not work today?

- Not all walls are used as fortresses. What are some walls that are built for pleasant purposes?

- When somebody says another person has built a wall between them, what does that mean?

Who Said That?

1. "I am the greatest."

2. "In Hartford, Hereford, and Hampshire, hurricanes hardly ever happen."

3. Who said, "That's one small step for man, one giant leap for mankind"?

4. "In the future everybody will be world-famous for fifteen minutes."

5. Who said, "It's not whether you get knocked down, it's whether you get up"?

6. Who quoted these lines from a Broadway musical when referring to her husband's administration: "Don't let it be forgot, that once there was a spot, for one brief shining moment that was known as Camelot"?

7. Who shouted these words at work at quitting time? "Yabba-dabba-doo!"

8. On which TV show did Michael Conrad's character, Sergeant Phil Esterhaus, tell his officers, "Let's be careful out there"?

9. Clara Peller was 83 years old when she became famous for saying "Where's the Beef?" What restaurant chain was she advertising for?

10. Who said, "I'm lucky...I have found my role...I love being with people"?

11. Who said, "Government is not the solution to our problem; government is the problem"?

12. "There is nothing wrong with America that cannot be cured by what is right with America."

Answers on page 128

Let's Talk

- Today we have many opportunities to read and watch what people say. Do you feel this enriches you?

- If you happen to like a famous person, are you more likely to believe the things he or she says? Can you think of a time when someone you did not like said something that impressed you?

- Has someone in your family surprised you by quoting you? Did you consider that a compliment? (We all have stories of how our children or kids in the family tossed our words back at us when we wished they had not.) Share yours with the group.

Who's the Boss?

1. What is the highest office in the United States?

2. Who presides over a court?

3. Name the person who is in charge of a class.

4. Who is the teacher's boss?

5. Even a city has a boss. Who is it?

6. The head person in the state is the…

7. The boss of a ship is who?

8. The boss of the airplane is who?

9. You may not see this person, but the train you ride has a boss. Who is this person?

10. You won't want to ever meet this boss, who is in charge of a prison.

11. An army lieutenant answers to the next rank up. Who is it?

12. The lowest commissioned officer in the navy is an…

Answers on page 128

Let's Talk

- There are good bosses and really awful bosses. Have everybody tell about some outstandingly good or bad bosses they have had.

- What are qualities you consider to be desirable in a boss?

- Some people think there should be no bosses and no rules. Why would this theory never work?

Who's the Boss? Bonus Questions

1. Jack Lemmon's line: "Captain, it is I, Ensign Pulver, and I just threw your stinking palm tree overboard." Who was the actor who played his boss?

2. You are an actor in a play. Who is your boss?

3. Vito Corleone was the undisputed boss of a crime family in what book and movie?

4. Mr. Spaceley was George's demanding boss on what animated TV series?

5. You play the violin in an orchestra. Who is your boss?

6. Which of the following is the boss: A seasoned newpaper reporter, or an editor one year out of college?

7. Which of the following is the boss: A newspaper editor with 24 years of experience, or a 24-year-old publisher who inherited the paper from his father?

8. Which of the following is the boss at an accident scene: An Emergency Medical Technician, or a police officer?

9. Who played radio station boss Arthur "Big Guy" Carlson in the TV sitcom *WKRP in Cincinnati*?

10. Mary Tyler Moore had a lovable grump for a boss in her 1970s TV series. Who played the role of Lou Grant?

11. For a while on the *Seinfeld* TV series, Elaine Benes worked for an eccentric catalog owner named J. Peterman. What actor, who later danced with the stars, played the part?

12. Moses was only following orders when he climbed up Mt. Sinai. Who was his boss?

Answers on page 128

Will Rogers Sayings

1. Live in such a way that you would not be ashamed to sell your parrot to the…

2. I joked about every prominent man in my lifetime, but I never met one I didn't…

3. A fool and his money are soon…

4. Everybody is ignorant. Only on different…

5. Everything is funny, as long as it's happening to…

6. An ignorant person is one who doesn't know what you have just…

7. Make crime pay. Become a…

8. My forefathers didn't come over on the Mayflower, but they…

9. I don't make jokes. I just watch the government and…

10. Don't let yesterday use up too much of…

11. All I know is what I read in the…

12. It's easy being a humorist when you've got the whole government working…

Answers on pages 128–129

Let's Talk

- Will Rogers' simplicity may have been his charm. He was accepted because he came across as a man of the common people. Would he have been so successful if he had worn a tuxedo and entertained in concert halls?

- Will Rogers was born in 1879 and he died in 1935, before World War II had even begun. Can you explain why his philosophies are considered quoteworthy today?

- Is there a public figure today that you especially enjoy listening to? Who is it and why is that person a favorite of yours?

Will Rogers Sayings Bonus Questions

1. Nothing you can't spell will ever...

2. I never expected to see the day when girls would get... in the places they do today.

3. The only time people dislike gossip is when you gossip about...

4. Diplomacy is the art of saying "Nice doggie" until you can find a...

5. Even if you're on the right track, you'll get run over if you just...

6. Be thankful we're not getting all the government we're...

7. The movies are the only business where you can go out front and applaud...

8. Politics is...

9. I belong to no organized party, I am a...

10. An onion can make people cry but there has never been a vegetable invented to make them...

11. The best doctor in the world is the veterinarian. He can't ask his patients what is the matter—he's got to just...

12. We can't all be heroes because somebody has to sit on the curb and clap as they...

Answers on page 129

William Shakespeare Quotes

1. Uneasy lies the head that wears a...

2. Brevity is the soul of...

3. Unbidden guests are often welcomest when they...

4. The first thing we do, let's kill all the...

5. Love comforteth like sunshine after...

6. It is a wise father that knows his own…

7. The wheel is come full…

8. The wheel that squeaks gets…

9. The Devil can cite Scripture for his…

10. The course of true love never did run…

11. Oh, Beware, My Lord, of jealousy. It is a green-eyed…

12. Lord, what fools we…

Answers on page 129

Let's Talk

- Shakespeare is one of the most quoted people in our culture. Some examples include the following: "It is a wise father that knows his own child," "To do a great right, do a little wrong," "As quiet as a lamb." Can you think of any more?

- *Romeo and Juliet* is one of Shakespeare's best-loved plays. Leonard Bernstein wrote the music for *West Side Story,* which was a successful Broadway show and movie based on those star-crossed lovers. Can you recall any of the famous songs?

- Do you have a favorite modern author that you believe will remain popular for a long time? Who is it? What did he or she write?

William Shakespeare Quotes Bonus Questions

1. I wasted time and now doth time…

2. We know what we are, but not what we…

3. While thou livest keep a good tongue in…

4. Nothing will come of…

5. A horse! A horse! My… for a horse!

6. Fire burn, and cauldron…

7. 'Tis neither here nor…

8. The law hath not been dead, though it hath...

9. What's mine is yours, and what is yours is...

10. I have not slept one...

11. In time we hate that which we often...

12. Good night sweet prince, and flights of angels sing thee to...

    Answers on page 129

Witches

1. Frank Sinatra's heart said, "yes indeed in me," so he gave up and told it to "proceed with what you're leading me to." What did he blame for that?

2. Samantha, the TV witch played by Elizabeth Montgomery, was the star in what TV show?

3. Samantha was married to Darrin. What was their last name?

4. In *The Wizard of Oz* a house fell on the Wicked Witch of the...

5. Among some primitive people, a person skilled in the art of healing is called a...

6. An extract made from bark and leaves of a small shrub with yellow flowers is used as an astringent. This liquid has a lady's name. What is it?

7. A "witch hunt" in 1692 resulted in trials of people accused of witchcraft. Where did that take place?

8. Sorcery and black magic are sometimes called what?

9. Glinda, the Good Witch of the North gave a pair of ruby slippers to whom?

10. Kim Novak played a witch with a lavendar cat in a movie called *Bell, Book, and...*?

11. Witches are often aided by a mysterious animal helper, such as a cat. What is the name given to this supernatural creature?

12. What is a male witch called?

    Answers on page 129

Let's Talk

- Even people who don't believe in witches often find the subject interesting. Do stories and movies about witches interest you? Why or why not?

- It would be an unusual Halloween party without at least one person showing up wearing a black cape and a black pointed hat. Besides witches being easily recognizable characters, why is that such an appealing costume?

- One witch we all know is The Wicked Witch of the West from *The Wizard of Oz*. We knew she was wicked from the moment she took Toto from Dorothy. Ironically Dorothy then got the ruby slippers from the clutches of the witch. Do you still enjoy watching the movie, even though you are now grown up?

Yellow

1. Another name for a wasp.

2. The sunflower is the official flower of what state?

3. Nebraska's official state flower grows wild, and it makes people with allergies sneeze. What it is?

4. If you call somebody "yellow" what are you accusing him of being?

5. A disease that can be spread by mosquitoes.

6. The Beatles said they lived in a very unusual yellow place in this 1966 song.

7. The nonsensical lyrics in a 1966 Donovan song refer to an electrical banana. What song is it?

8. It was an "Itsy Bitsy Teenie Weenie…

9. Tony Orlando said he did his time and was coming home. What did he want her to do?

10. Joni Mitchell said "Late last night I heard the screen door slam." Then, what took away her old man?

11. What is the name of crocus stigmas after they are dried and used for cooking?

12. Bile pigments in the blood cause the eyeballs and skin to be yellow. What is this condition called?

Answers on page 129

Let's Talk

• Name some yellow objects that are important in your life.

• Yellow is considered a happy color. If you are feeling tired or just not your best, do you find that wearing something yellow will make you feel better? Would you like a yellow kitchen?

• Ask everybody to think of a few things that you would definitely not want to be yellow.

Selected Print Resources

Agay, D. (1975). *Best loved songs of the American people.* Garden City, NY: GuildAmerica Books.

Agnes, M. (Ed.). (2003). *Webster's new world dictionary* (4th ed.). New York, NY: Pocket Books.

Bartlett, J. (1980). *Familiar quotations* (15th and 125th anniversary edition). Boston, MA: Little, Brown and Company.

Berkow, R. et al. (Ed.). (1997). *Merck manual of medical information, home edition.* Whitehouse Station, NJ: Merck & Co.

Bridgwater, W. (Ed.). (1953). *The Columbia–Viking desk encyclopedia.* New York, NY: Viking Press.

Chapman, R. L. (n.d.). *Roget's international thesaurus* (4th ed.). New York, NY: Thomas Y. Crowell.

Fardnon, J. et al. (1998). *Giant book of questions and answers.* Great Britain: Dempsey-Parr.

Frey, H. (Ed.). (1935). *America sings, community song book.* New York, NY: Robbins Music Corporation.

Freedman, G. (Ed.). (1962). *Mitch Miller community song book.* New York, NY: Warner Bros, Inc.

Holy Bible, Authorized King James Version. New York, NY: Harper & Brothers Publishers.

Kenyon, S. (1994). *The writer's digest character naming sourcebook.* Cincinnati, OH: Writer's Digest Books.

Landau, S. I. and Bogus, R. J. (Eds.). (1975). *The doubleday dictionary for home, school, and office.* Garden City, NY: Doubleday & Company.

Maltin, L. (Ed.). (2001). *Leonard Maltin's movie and video guide.* New York, NY: Plume Book.

MacMillan Literature Series. (1991). *Understanding literature.* Mission Hills, CA: Glencoe-McGraw-Hill.

Our American century, 100 years of Hollywood. (n.d.). Alexandria, VA: Time-Life Books.

Our American century, decade of triumph—the 40s. (n.d.). Alexandria, VA: Time-Life Books.

Our American century, events that shaped the century. (n.d.). Alexandria, VA: Time-Life Books.

Our American century, hard times. (n.d.). Alexandria, VA: Time-Life Books.

Our American century, pride and prosperity—the 80s. (n.d.). Alexandria, VA: Time-Life Books.

Our American century, rock and roll generation—teen life in the 50s. (n.d.). Alexandria, VA: Time-Life Books.

Our American century, the American dream—the 50s. (n.d.). Alexandria, VA: Time-Life Books.

Our American century, the digital decade—the 90s. (n.d.). Alexandria, VA: Time-Life Books.

Our American century, the jazz age. (n.d.). Alexandria, VA: Time-Life Books.

Our American century, turbulent years—the 60s. (n.d.). Alexandria, VA: Time-Life Books.

Rombauer, I. and Becker, M. R. (1980). *Joy of Cooking.* Indianapolis, IN: The Bobbs-Merrill Company.

Thorndike, E. L. (1957). *Thorndike–Barnhart advanced junior dictionary.* Chicago, IL: Scott, Foresman and Company.

Understanding literature. (1991). Mission Hills: Glencoe-McGraw-Hill.

Vetter, J. (2002). *Heroes.* Mt. Airy, MD: ElderSong Publications.

Wallechinsky, D. and Wallace, I. (1975). *The people's almanac.* Garden City, NY: Doubleday & Company.

Worth, Fred L. (n.d.). *The complete unabridged super trivia encyclopedia.* Los Angeles, CA: Brooke House.

Selected Online Resources

http://aolsuc.digitalcity.com/stlouis/entertainment/venue
http://ask.yahoo.com/ask/20000216.html
http://catalogue.deccaclassics.com/catalogue/prodshow.jsp?searchstr=448957
http://cgfa.floridaimaging.com/gainsboro
http://classics.www5.50megs.com/jstewartbio.htm
http://composite.about.com/library/glossary/f/bldef-f2265.ht
http://en.wikipedia.org/wiki/Jimmy_Swaggart
http://en.wikipedia.org/wiki/Peace_Bridge
http://hub/org/reaings/st.louis.blues.htnl
http://info.net/.HITS/1939.html
http://info.net/.hits/1944.html
http://ingeb.org/songs/greengre.html
http://joan-of-arc.org/joanofarc_short_biography.html
http://law.umkc.edu/faculty/projects/ftrials/hauptmann/bruno.html
http://law.umkc.edu/faculty/projects/ftrials/reosenberg/r
http://limoservicerome.com/vaticansightseeingtours
http://littlebrownchurch.org
http://maninblack.net/lyrics/MAN%20IN%20BLACK.htm
http://margaritaville.com/
http://money.cnn.com/2003/05/13/news/economy/twenty
http://www.Moscow-hotels-russia.com/vasil_blagen.htm

http://music.channel.aol.com/artist/artistbio.adp?artistid=1795
http://my.unidata.ucar.edu/content/staff/blynds/rnbw.htm
http://www.npwrc.usgs.govhelp/faq/animals/names.htm
http://search.eb.com/titanic/01_01.html
http://statelibrary.dcr.state.nc.us/nc/bio/literary/murrow.htm
http://stjude.tv/danny_thomas_story.cfm
http://suvcw.org/gar.htm
http://timstvshowcase.com/kangaroo.html
http://timvp.com/dannyt.html
http://users.adelphia.net/~rli/bookstore.html
http://ww.kithrup.com/àriyana/maewest/html
http://www. classicthemes.com/50sTVthemes/theme
http://www.7up.com/index.aspx
http://www.able2know.com/forums/about28019-0-asc-10.html
http://www.achievement.org
http://www.achooallergy.com
http://www.airpower.maxwell.af.mil/airchronicles/cc/doo.html
http://www.amazon.com/exec/obidos/tg/detail/-/0345348109?v=glance
http://www.aolsvc.worldbook.aol.com
http://www.aria.co.nz/billboard/50s_yearly_top_40.html
http://www.aria.co.nz/billboard/70s_yearly_top_40.html
http://www.aria.co.nz/billboard/50s_yearly_top_40.html
http://www.aria.co.nz/billboard/60s_yearly_top_40.html
http://www.aria.co.nz/billboard/70s_yearly_top_40.html
http://www.arlingtoncemetery.net/jfk.htm
http://www.artencylopeda.com
http://www.awildorchid.com/monuments.htm
http://www.bcdb.com/bcdb/detailed.cgi?film=3820
http://www.biography.com/features/awards/supactor.html
http://www.brainyquote.com/quotes/authors/will_rogers.html
http://www.cdc.gov/malaria/history/panama_canal.htm
http://www.cliffsnotes.com/WileyCDA/LitNote/id-79,pageNum-5.html
http://www.clogdancing.com/
http://www.cmt.com/artists/news/1473148/06232003/page_patti.jhtm
http://www.cnn.com/WORLD/9709/mother.teresa/
http://www.contemplator.com/america/lilacs.html
http://www.corfid.com/gl/wreck.htm
http://www.dailysoft.com/berlinwall/history/berlinwall-timeline.htm
http://www.ddavid.com/formula1/story.htm
http://www.desertusa.com/july97/du_bwindow.html
http://www.digitaldreamdoor.com/pages/quoes/maewest.html

http://www.djmorton.demon.co.uk/scouting/songs/unicorn.htm
http://www.dosado.com/articles/hist-maca.html
http://www.doyourownpestcontrol.com
http://www.elyrics4u.com
http://www.fas.org/man/dod-101/sys/ship/sullivans.htm
http://www.geocities.com/~charrstarr/rb/j/jimmy_mack.html
http://www.geocities.com/Broadway/Lobby/1009/book2/k61.htm
http://www.geocities.com/Broadway/Lobby/1009/trhk/trhk35.htm
http://www.geocities.com/Hollywood/Park/1568/AngelswithDirtyFaces.htm
http://www.geocities.com/TelevisionCity/2420/cast.html
http://www.gmcanada.com/english/vehicles/gmc/jimmy/jimm_overview.html
http://www.gp.org/
http://www.great-britain.co.uk/regions/scots_english%20border/hadrians.ht
http://www.habitat.org/jcwp/2000/
http://www.heptune.com/preslist.html
http://www.historicstjohnschurch.org/pages/history.htm
http://www.history.navy.mil/photos/events/wwii-pac/japansur/js-8c.htm
http://www.h-net.org/reviews/showpdf.cgi?path=26261069470455
http://www.holidays.net/father/story.htm
http://www.ibiblio.org/john_henry/other.html
http://www.ilr.cornell.edu/trianglefire/
http://www.imdb.com/title/tt0055660/
http://www.innotts.co.uk/asperges/george/george2.html
http://www.jcu.edu.au/school/phtm/PHTM/hlice/hlinfo1.htm
http://www.jwplace.com/tour.html
http://www.loc.gov/exhibits/gadd/images/frstdrt1.jpg
http://www.lyricsfreak.com
http://www.lyricsondemand.com/k/kennyrogerslyrics/islandsinthestreamlyr-
ics.html
http://www.mayflowerhistory.com/History/voyage_secondary.php
http://www.metrolyrics.com/lyrics/158147/Frank_Sinatra/Birth_of_The_
Blues
http://www.michaelflatley.com/
http://www.midisite.co.uk/midi_search/pomp.html
http://www.multied.com/Bio/presidents/nixon.html
http://www.museum.tv/archives
http://www.musicradio77.com
http://www.nacsonline.com
http://www.naglefarms.com/Movie.html
http://www.nationalgeographic.com/railroad/j2.html
http://www.newsday.com/news/columnists/ny-jimmybreslin.columnist

http://www.nps.gov
http://www.nytimes.com/library/review/082000forest-fires-r
http://www.olivebranch.com/isreal/jesurwall.htm
http://www.online-literature.com
http://www.orkin.com
http://www.pbs.org/wgbh/amex/dillinger/filmmore/ps_confess.html
http://www.ronscurrency.com/ronef.htm
http://www.sesame-encyclopedia.com/Alphabet/SesameB/Bert.html
http://www.sheppardsoftware.com/dynamic_MC_Animal_Trivia_web.html
http://www.si.edu/resource/faq/nmnh/famehors.htm
http://www.songlyrics4u.com
http://www.spartacus.schoolnet.co.uk/USAhoffa.htm
http://www.states.com/flower.htm
http://www.state-tree.com
http://www.straightdope.com/classics/a2_250
http://www.templeinstitute.org/artiles/Solomons-Temple.html
http://www.terrace.qld.edu.au/academic/lote/french/yr5cous.htm
http://www.theculturedtraveler.com/Archives/JUL2004/Lead_Story.h
http://www.themick.com/
http://www.thesonglyrics.com/d_song_lyrics/johndenver_lyric2.html
http://www.thingstodo-london/brochure/content
http://www.travel.spb.ru/
http://www.unesco.org/sites/252.htm
http://www.usahistory.info/south/Arnold.html
http://www.usatrivia.com/pasnatt.html
http://www.webfitz.com/lyrics/Lyrics/1968/231968.html
http://www.weeuniverse.com
http://www.westminster-abbey.org
http://www.whitehouse.gov/history/presidents
http://www.yellowstoneparknet.com
http://www1.minn.net/~keithp/ships.htm
http:the-colosseum.net/idx-en.htm
http:www.japanorama.com/kyuchan.html

Answers

All Dressed Up
1. tutu
2. habit
3. ruff
4. bustle
5. hoop
6. apron
7. kimono
8. toga
9. leotards
10. sari
11. veil
12. scrubs

All Dressed Up Bonus Questions
1. spats
2. bib
3. vest
4. ice skates
5. jodhpurs or riding pants
6. shower cap
7. suspenders
8. leg warmers
9. diaper
10. wet suit
11. cleats
12. bandanna

Angels
1. egg whites
2. fear to go (tread)
3. guardian angel
4. Red Tail Angels
5. Gabriel
6. cherubim
7. twelve
8. devil
9. *Angels With Dirty Faces*
10. money
11. sing
12. Battle of Gettysburg

Animal Friends
1. dingo
2. tusk
3. females
4. 600
5. humans
6. ostrich
7. piranha
8. earthworm
9. hummingbird
10. saliva
11. sea horses
12. viper

Animals Getting Together
1. gaggle or flock
2. troop
3. swarm
4. string, stable, or herd
5. a school, draft, or shoal
6. herd or drovel
7. pride
8. yoke, drove, or herd
9. sloth or sleuth
10. herd or parade
11. cloud, horde, or swarm
12. pod or herd

Bad Guys and Gals
1. Lizzie Borden
2. Bonnie and Clyde
3. George "Machine Gun" Kelly
4. Pretty Boy Floyd
5. Ma Barker
6. John Dillinger
7. Baby Face Nelson
8. Ethel and Julius Rosenberg
9. Bruno Richard Hauptmann
10. Billy the Kid
11. Charles Starkweather
12. Al Capone

Begins With "be"
1. behave
2. beguile
3. begrudge
4. begin
5. beholden
6. being
7. before
8. behalf
9. begone
10. behind
11. behest
12. behold

Begins with "em"
1. employ
2. Auntie Em
3. emote
4. emerald
5. emigrates
6. emphasis
7. employee
8. empty
9. embroidery
10. embezzle
11. embrace
12. emu

Black
1. Johnny Cash
2. black jack
3. black magic
4. black-hearted
5. blackout
6. blacksmith
7. black widow
8. black hole
9. blacklist
10. black sheep
11. black eye
12. black-eyed Susan

Blue
1. unexpected
2. *Lady Sings the Blues*
3. indigo
4. "Learnin' the Blues"
5. "Honky Tonk Blues"
6. "Song Sung Blue"
7. "Birth of the Blues"
8. *The Blue Boy*
9. *The Blue Angel*
10. Scarlett and Rhett Butler
11. The Blues Brothers
12. a mold, or fungus

Body Parts
1. heart
2. mouth (a tooth)
3. brushing
4. nose
5. skin
6. 98.6 degrees Fahrenheit
7. knit
8. *Cool Hand Luke*
9. appendix
10. nose
11. finger
12. head

Bookish Words
1. bookmark
2. matchbook
3. bookie, or bookmaker
4. bookshelf, or bookcase
5. bookworm
6. bookish
7. bookmobile
8. bookkeeper
9. bookends
10. book
11. bookplate
12. bookbinder

Bridges
1. "Bridge Over Troubled Water"
2. burned your bridges
3. natural teeth
4. nose
5. Brooklyn Bridge
6. Verrazano-Narrows Bridge
7. *The Bridges at Toko-Ri*
8. *The Bridges of Madison County*
9. *The Bridge on the River Kwai*
10. Peace Bridge
11. whist
12. strings

Celebrity Quotes
1. Theodore Roosevelt
2. John F. Kennedy
3. Yogi Berra
4. Anne Frank
5. J. Edgar Hoover
6. Abraham Lincoln
7. Richard Nixon
8. Winston Churchill
9. Vince Lombardi
10. W. C. Fields
11. Muhammad Ali
12. Brando *(On the Waterfront)*

Chapels and Places of Worship
1. The Colosseum
2. cruciform
3. Westminster Abbey
4. St. Paul's Cathedral
5. The Sistine Chapel
6. "The Little Brown Church in the Wildwood"
7. Taj Mahal
8. St. Basil's Cathedral
9. The Alamo
10. St. John's Episcopal Church, formerly Anglican

11. altar/pulpit
12. "The Chapel of Love"

Comic Strip Characters
1. Catwoman
2. Li'l Abner
3. Woody Woodpecker
4. Mr. Dithers
5. *The Daily Planet,* formerly *The Daily Star*
6. Lois Lane
7. Dick Tracy
8. Dick Tracy
9. Donald Duck, Huey, Dewey, and Louie
10. Wonder Woman
11. Spider-man
12. Batman

Comparisons to Animals
1. stool pigeon
2. chicken
3. jackass
4. book worm
5. cold turkey
6. catty
7. piggish
8. rabbit
9. slothful
10. elephant
11. mule
12. lion

Comparisons to Animals Bonus Questions
1. fish
2. flea
3. gazelle
4. cat
5. owl
6. hen

7. beaver, or bee
8. snake
9. kitten
10. dodo
11. pig
12. cow

7. *The Danny Thomas Show*
8. Elton John
9. Kaye
10. DeVito
11. Daniel
12. The Den of Lions

Couples
1. Ozzie Nelson, Ricky Nelson
2. Tonto
3. Dale Evans
4. Wild Bill Hickok
5. Paul Newman
6. Ken
7. Olive Oyl
8. Donny and Marie Osmond
9. Wilma
10. Clark
11. Maid Marian
12. Tarzan

Dancing
1. belly dance
2. The Twist
3. tap dancing
4. clogging
5. Fred Astaire and Ginger Rogers
6. hula
7. The Hokey Pokey
8. "Dancing Queen"
9. ballet
10. square dance
11. Ireland
12. handkerchief dance

Creepy, Crawly Bugs
1. mosquito
2. black widow spider
3. ladybug
4. cicada
5. ant
6. louse
7. flea
8. cockroach
9. termite
10. bed bugs
11. dust mite
12. entomology

Devils
1. dust devils
2. Diablo
3. devil-may-care
4. the devil
5. Devil's Island
6. devil fish
7. devilish
8. devil's advocate
9. devil's advocate
10. Devil's Tower
11. The Phantom
12. …behind me Satan

Dan and Danny and Daniel
1. Dan Patch
2. Danny Thomas
3. "Cool Water"
4. *Dan August*
5. Briggs
6. Mark Twain

Dogs
1. Chips
2. Snoopy
3. Balto
4. Bowser
5. Buck
6. Checkers

7. toy
8. The Farmer in the Dell
9. Lyndon B. Johnson
10. Liberty
11. *Lady and the Tramp*
12. King

Ends with "ate"
1. accentuate
2. acclimate
3. arbitrate
4. celebrate
5. compensate
6. complicate
7. adulterate
8. commiserate
9. concentrate
10. associate
11. consolidate
12. inundate

Ends With "ate" Bonus Questions
1. graduate
2. decimate
3. decorate
4. delegate
5. educate
6. emancipate
7. emigrate
8. evaporate
9. fascinate
10. negotiate
11. indicate
12. delineate

Ends With "ute"
1. compute
2. cute
3. brute
4. jute
5. mute
6. hirsute

7. lute
8. absolute
9. dispute
10. flute
11. acute
12. astute

Ends With "ute" Bonus Questions
1. route
2. salute
3. pollute
4. commute
5. repute
6. depute
7. dilute
8. execute
9. prosecute
10. involute
11. minute
12. minute

Family Names
1. Clampett
2. Mitchell
3. Richards
4. Corleone
5. Cleaver
6. Cartwright
7. Brady
8. Kramden
9. Norton
10. Ricardo
11. Williams
12. Partridge

Family Ties
1. *Mommie Dearest*
2. Mother Teresa
3. fathers
4. "Whistler's Mother"
5. President George Bush and his son George W. Bush

6. maternal grandfather of John Kennedy
7. *Father of the Bride*
8. Mother's Day
9. "Oh, My Papa"
10. her grandson
11. The Sullivans
12. cousins

Famous Doctors
1. Dr. Henry Jekyll
2. Dr. Christiaan Barnard
3. Milburn Stone
4. Ben Casey
5. Dr. Zorba
6. Dr. Jonas Salk
7. Dr. Doolittle
8. Dr. James Kildare
9. James Brolin
10. Dr. Pepper
11. Dr. Seuss
12. Chad Everett

Famous Ships
1. *Titanic*
2. *USS Missouri*
3. John F. Kennedy
4. *The Edmund Fitzgerald*
5. *Moby Dick*
6. *The Mayflower*
7. *The Jolly Roger*
8. Francis Scott Key
9. *Santa Maria*
10. *USS Arizona*
11. *The Vulture*
12. *The Queen Anne's Revenge*

Finish the Slogan
1. place
2. Allstate
3. someone
4. Chevrolet

5. just one
6. Hawaiian Punch
7. R-O-L-A-I-D-S
8. sometimes you don't
9. the very best
10. buck or two
11. O-S-C-A-R, M-A-Y-E-R
12. varieties

Finish the Slogan Bonus Questions
1. picker upper
2. do ya
3. by name
4. Sure
5. New York
6. want to be
7. champions
8. time
9. Charmin
10. worth it
11. together
12. Bud's

Fire and Heat
1. fire
2. heat wave
3. a lantern
4. firefly, or lightning bug
5. "Burning Love"
6. sulfur
7. heat lightning
8. Triangle Shirt-Waist Factory
9. flash point
10. Richmond
11. The Eternal Flame
12. "Light My Fire"

Firsts
1. Eleanor Roosevelt
2. Mickey Mouse
3. Jacques Cousteau
4. Jackie Robinson

5. Chuck Yeager
6. Glenn Miller
7. Edward R. Murrow
8. Lucille Ball
9. Babe Ruth
10. Medicare
11. Richard M. Nixon
12. Thomas Alva Edison

Foreign Language Hits
1. *La Bamba*
2. "Mañana"
3. "Auf Wiederseh'n, Sweetheart"
4. "Vaya Con Dios"
5. "Eh Cumpari"
6. "C'est Si Bon"
7. "Que Sera Sera"
8. "Volare"
9. "Sayonara"
10. "Hava Nagila"
11. "Frère Jacques"
12. "Sukiyaki"

Forgetting and Remembering
1. forget-me-not
2. Remember Pearl Harbor
3. Remember the *Maine*
4. Remember the Alamo
5. Gettysburg Address
6. The Sabbath Day
7. an elephant
8. make an exception
9. forgotten himself
10. remember him
11. "Give My Regards to Broadway"
12. Red River Valley

Green
1. "The Ballad of the Green Berets"
2. yellow and blue
3. "The Green Door"
4. "Greenfields"

5. Little Green Apples
6. chlorophyll
7. The Green Party
8. "The Green, Green Grass of Home"
9. Greenland
10. green-eyed monster
11. "Green Grow the Lilacs"
12. greenhouse gases

Hair-Hair
1. crew cut
2. pompadour
3. hirsute
4. toupee
5. a hair trigger
6. hairballs
7. hairdo
8. hair stylist, or hairdresser
9. barber
10. hair-raising
11. hairsbreadth
12. splitting hairs

Head Wear
1. dunce cap
2. Easter bonnet
3. 10-gallon hat
4. wimple
5. baseball cap
6. helmet
7. derby
8. tam-o-shanter, or tam
9. visor, or bill
10. crown
11. stocking cap
12. beret

Hills and Mountains
1. "Blueberry Hill"
2. "She'll Be Comin' Round the Mountain"

3. "Mockin' Bird Hill"
4. Fujiyama, or Mount Fuji
5. Old Smokey
6. The Matterhorn
7. "Rocky Mountain High"
8. Spencer's Mountain (the TV series *The Waltons* referred to it as Walton's Mountain)
9. Appalachian Mountains
10. Mount Everest
11. The Bighorn Mountains
12. Little Round Top

Hollywood Hunks
1. Clint Eastwood
2. Paul Newman, Robert Redford
3. Sidney Poitier
4. Harrison Ford (Indiana Jones)
5. John Wayne
6. Charlton Heston (Moses)
7. Johnny Weissmuller (Tarzan)
8. Christopher Reeve (Superman)
9. Gary Cooper (*High Noon*)
10. Warren Beatty
11. James Dean (*Rebel Without a Cause*)
12. Cary Grant (*North by Northwest*)

Horses
1. Trigger
2. John F. Kennedy
3. Paul Revere
4. Calico
5. Gene Autry
6. Clydesdale
7. Ascot
8. Duke
9. The Four Horsemen of the Apocalypse
10. Cochise
11. The Pie
12. left

House Sweet Home
1. glass houses
2. White House
3. courthouse
4. sorority house
5. *Animal House*
6. penthouse
7. condominium
8. duplex
9. warehouse
10. doghouse
11. igloo
12. tent

Initials
1. Mobile Army Surgical Hospital
2. Metro Goldwyn Mayer
3. before Christ
4. British Columbia
5. United Kingdom
6. 1,000
7. Los Angeles, Louisiana
8. Central Intelligence Agency
9. Parent Teacher Association
10. intelligence quotient
11. Federal Bureau of Investigation
12. before noon

Instrumentally Speaking
1. trombone
2. reed
3. flute
4. guitar
5. banjo
6. drum
7. tambourine
8. tuba
9. whistle
10. woodwind
11. violin, viola, cello, stand-up bass
12. harp (Harpo)

Islands
1. *Island in the Sun*
2. *Islands in the Stream*
3. "Islands in the Stream"
4. Alcatraz
5. Hawaii
6. Mediterranean
7. Canada
8. Australia
9. Long Island
10. Cuba
11. California
12. Iwo Jima

It's About Time
1. grandfather clock
2. wristwatch
3. "Rock Around the Clock"
4. clock/radio
5. Big Ben
6. sundial
7. time clock
8. daylight savings time
9. kitchen timer
10. stopwatch
11. pocket watch
12. hourglass

It's Grand
1. grandmother
2. grand piano
3. grand jury
4. grand slam
5. grandeur
6. grandchild
7. Grand Canyon
8. grand uncle
9. Grand Prix
10. Grand Tetons
11. Grand Coulee Dam
12. Grand Army of the Republic

Jimmy
1. President Jimmy Carter
2. crowbar
3. Jimmy Buffett
4. Jimmie Rodgers
5. Jimmy Stewart
6. Jimmy Breslin
7. General Jimmy Doolittle
8. "Jimmy Mack"
9. Jimmy Swaggart
10. Jimmy Hoffa
11. Jimmy Cagney
12. GMC Jimmy

John and Jack
1. John F. Kennedy, Jr.
2. John Adams
3. jack-in-the-box
4. jack boot
5. jackknife
6. Jack Frost
7. jackrabbit
8. jacks
9. John Doe
10. Johnny Appleseed
11. John Henry
12. John F. Kennedy

Let's Celebrate
1. St. Valentine's Day
2. Ramadan
3. Mother's Day
4. Rosh Hashana
5. Yom Kippur
6. the first Monday in September
7. the last Monday in May
8. New Year's Day
9. the third
10. Thanksgiving
11. President's Day
12. Martin Luther King, Jr.'s birthday

Let's Sit Down
1. high chair
2. rocking chair
3. reclining chair
4. pew
5. bench
6. potty chair
7. wheelchair
8. love seat
9. throne
10. electric chair
11. easy chair
12. chairman, chairwoman, or chair

Lucky Sevens
1. 7
2. The Seven Deadly Sins
3. The Seven Dwarfs
4. *The Seven Little Foys*
5. South Pacific
6. temperance
7. The Seven Wonders of the World
8. dead
9. Watergate Seven
10. Seventh Heaven
11. Rome
12. Mickey Mantle

Mae West Wit: Finish the Quote
1. the stork.
2. imported.
3. better.
4. better.
5. in the street.
6. drifted.
7. right after her.
8. chickadee
9. in love.
10. diamond.
11. reform schools are for.
12. see me sometime.

Mae West Wit: Finish the Quote Bonus Questions
1. keep you.
2. an umbrella.
3. wages of sin.
4. overlooked.
5. life in my men.
6. an institution yet.
7. don't break any.
8. multitude of sins.
9. bad girls found out.
10. still got them.
11. wonderful.
12. I never tried yet.

Money, Money, Money
1. *Pennies From Heaven*
2. A penny for your thoughts.
3. Ulysses S. Grant
4. Andrew Jackson
5. George Washington
6. five cents
7. ten cents
8. numismatist
9. millionaire
10. Wall Street
11. a bell
12. all evil

Nicknames
1. Bruce Springsteen
2. The It Girl
3. Latin Lover
4. Man of a Thousand Faces
5. The Duke
6. James Bond
7. Joe DiMaggio
8. Tokyo Rose
9. Axis Sally
10. George Herman "Babe" Ruth
11. Milton Berle
12. Blackbeard

Not People
1. a horse
2. *Of Mice and Men*
3. *Pete's Dragon*
4. an orca, or killer whale
5. Peter Rabbit
6. *The Pink Panther*
7. Pinocchio
8. a mouse
9. a deer
10. "Puff, the Magic Dragon"
11. Teddy Bear
12. "The Unicorn"

Old Sayings, Part One
1. the grease
2. your friend
3. shame on me
4. scorned
5. weep alone
6. soon parted
7. can't afford it
8. the rest of your life
9. fleas
10. give me death
11. fade away
12. public places

Old Sayings, Part Two
1. to drive
2. twice a day
3. "I don't want to"
4. probably is
5. spots
6. calm
7. may get it
8. done anything
9. a pound of cure
10. put it back in
11. him one of yours
12. all doubt

Old Sayings, Part Three
1. buttered on
2. never done
3. the piper
4. dealt
5. never to have tried at all
6. crumbles
7. whites of their eyes
8. gifts
9. top
10. level
11. valor
12. chew

Old Sayings, Part Four
1. eleven
2. shines on
3. sailors' delight
4. weakest link
5. dangerous thing
6. problems
7. mountains
8. thankless child
9. the beholder
10. horse is out
11. other side of the fence
12. never win

One Hundred
1. a hymn
2. Sleeping Beauty
3. the secret word
4. *101 Dalmatians*
5. Hundred Acre Wood
6. 10
7. centenarian
8. centennial
9. 100
10. Thomas Jefferson (for those who said Mark Twain, you're close. He said, "When angry,

count four; when very angry, swear."

11. hardest
12. 20th century

One Name is Enough

1. Houdini
2. Marconi
3. Curie
4. Berlin
5. Wilson
6. Carver
7. Chaplin
8. Rickenbacher
9. Gandhi
10. Freud
11. Theodore
12. Ford

Oscar Loves the Ladies

1. Ellen Burstyn, in *Alice Doesn't Live Here Anymore*
2. Ingrid Bergman, in *Anastasia*
3. Jodie Foster
4. Cher, in *Moonstruck*
5. *Misery*
6. Helen Hunt
7. Anne Bancroft, in *The Miracle Worker*
8. Jessica Tandy, in *Driving Miss Daisy*
9. Holly Hunter
10. Susan Sarandon
11. Julia Roberts
12. Louise Fletcher

Oscar's Songs

1. *The Big Broadcast of 1938*
2. "Colors of the Wind"
3. "Mona Lisa"
4. "Evergreen"
5. "Moon River"

6. "White Christmas"
7. "Swinging on a Star"
8. "The Morning After"
9. "Zip-A-Dee-Doo-Dah"
10. "It Might As Well Be Spring"
11. "You Light Up My Life"
12. "Up Where We Belong"

Our Funny Language

1. USO (United Service Organization)
2. scat singing
3. cut a rug
4. canaries
5. hamburger
6. hot rod
7. bread
8. kick
9. bam boom
10. kicks
11. OK
12. the Internet

Patriotic Songs

1. "Stars and Stripes Forever"
2. "Yankee Doodle"
3. "The Battle Hymn of the Republic"
4. *Yankee Doodle Dandy*
5. "God Bless America"
6. "You're a Grand Old Flag"
7. "The Caissons Go Rolling Along"
8. "Dixie"
9. "Pomp and Circumstance"
10. "The Washington Post March"
11. "The Star Spangled Banner" (Oh, say can you see?)
12. "America the Beautiful"

Presidential Peculiarities

1. Harry S. Truman
2. Earl

3. Ronald Reagan
4. Abraham Lincoln
5. Richard Nixon
6. Theodore Roosevelt
7. James Buchanan
8. William Howard Taft
9. Grover Cleveland
10. Gerald Ford
11. all were named James
12. Ronald Reagan

Queens and Kings
1. ABBA
2. King Arthur
3. "King of the Road"
4. The African Queen
5. King Edward VIII
6. Queen Elizabeth II
7. Grace Kelly
8. Britain
9. King Kong
10. Billy Jean King
11. The Queen Mary
12. Queen Anne's Lace

Red
1. cheeks, or face
2. redwood, or sequoia
3. A
4. ruby
5. ruby slippers
6. a red cap
7. John Dillinger
8. shoes
9. anemia
10. China
11. British
12. failing

Rock
1. pet rocks
2. Plymouth

3. rules the world
4. Rock-a-Bye Baby
5. the rocks
6. rockabilly
7. diamonds
8. lava
9. Rock of Gibraltar
10. ice
11. "Rock Around the Clock"
12. Alcatraz

Saints Go Marching
1. "When the Saints Go Marching In"
2. St. Joan of Arc
3. St. Joseph's Day
4. St. Petersberg
5. St. Petersberg
6. Ireland
7. St. George
8. The Saint Valentine's Day Massacre
9. The Virgin Islands
10. St. John
11. St. Louis, Missouri
12. "St. Louis Blues," or "St. Louis Woman"

Ships and Boats
1. *The Caine Mutiny*
2. "Proud Mary"
3. states
4. *The Sloop John B*
5. *Mutiny on the Bounty*
6. *Show Boat*
7. cities
8. American naval heroes
9. fish
10. *The Sand Pebbles*
11. pirogue
12. *The Bounty*

Shoes: What Kind?
1. white buckskin shoes
2. blue suede shoes
3. ruby slippers
4. wooden shoes, clogs, klompen
5. wedgies
6. thongs
7. sandal
8. moccasins
9. sneakers
10. getting booted
11. booties
12. toe shoes, or pointe shoes

Shoes Bonus Questions
1. midnight
2. buckles
3. aglet
4. gumshoe
5. sneakers
6. insoles
7. wings
8. bound
9. so many children she didn't know what to do
10. elevator shoes
11. wing tip
12. steel toe shoes

Skin
1. beauty
2. skin-tight
3. skin-flint
4. skin-diving
5. skinner
6. mule skinner
7. skinny
8. skin
9. paper
10. chameleon
11. Martin Luther King, Jr.
12. snake

Slogans and Mottos
1. not war
2. do ya
3. taste good
4. Budweiser
5. Be Prepared.
6. infamy
7. 4-H Club
8. Why
9. last drop
10. In God We Trust
11. who owns one
12. Doublemint Gum

Slogans and Mottos Bonus Questions
1. Camel
2. baby (Virginia Slims)
3. Phillip Morris
4. ordered (L&M Cigarettes)
5. cough (Old Gold)
6. Winston
7. Lucky
8. Camels
9. Camels
10. Strand
11. Tiparillo
12. Mail Pouch

Stars
1. "Don't Let the Stars Get in Your Eyes"
2. the evening star
3. red (the red planet)
4. dust
5. the moon
6. twinkling
7. air
8. refraction
9. the sun
10. astronomer

11. *A Star is Born*
12. Milky Way

Suns and Moons
1. it's orbit is not perfectly circular
2. "Sundown"
3. "Sunshine On My Shoulder"
4. is never done
5. *Sunrise at Campobello*
6. "We'll Sing in the Sunshine"
7. "You Are My Sunshine"
8. Neil Armstrong
9. Earth's shadow
10. holes
11. *The Sunshine Boys*
12. moonshine

Tom and Thomas
1. Thomas Jefferson (The Declaration of Independence)
2. cat
3. Tom Turkey
4. tomahawk
5. tomboy
6. Tom Sawyer
7. Tom and Jerry
8. General Tom Thumb
9. Tom Jones
10. Thomas Dewey
11. Doubting Thomas
12. Tom Terrific

Trains
1. The Monkees
2. kitten
3. "I've Been Working on the Railroad"
4. "The Trolley Song"
5. Promontory Point, Utah
6. *Murder on the Orient Express*

7. *The Train*
8. "Chattanooga Choo-Choo"
9. "Casey Jones"
10. Harriet Tubman
11. Pullman car
12. caboose

Trees and Flowers
1. *The Days of Wine and Roses*
2. "Flowers on the Wall"
3. "You Don't Bring Me Flowers"
4. *Flower Drum Song*
5. white ash
6. paper
7. baskets
8. water lily
9. opium poppy
10. sugar maple
11. California redwood
12. wanted

TV Characters
1. Clarabelle
2. Dick Clark
3. Ben Casey
4. Marcus Welby
5. Roy Clark
6. Ernie
7. Mr. Green Jeans
8. *The Partridge Family*
9. Sergeant Joe Friday
10. "Doc" Galen Adams
11. "Heeeeeeeere's Johnny"
12. Andy Williams

Twain-isms
1. not obliged to do
2. the truth
3. needs to
4. swear
5. children

6. in Hell
7. astonish the rest
8. it was forbidden
9. the work
10. has only nine lives
11. bother
12. I didn't know

Twain-isms Bonus Questions
1. misprint
2. absence of fear
3. here first
4. money in it
5. actually happened
6. resting
7. education
8. not deserve them
9. so rare
10. succeed
11. laughter
12. yourself

Walls
1. Wailing Wall, or Western Wall
2. Berlin Wall
3. The Great Wall of China
4. The Vietnam Memorial
5. Britain
6. drive them up the wall
7. Humpty Dumpty
8. Jackson
9. Moses
10. Wall Street
11. Jericho
12. Trojan Horse

Who Said That?
1. Muhammad Ali
2. Eliza Doolittle, or Prof. Henry Higgins *(My Fair Lady)*
3. Neil Armstrong
4. Andy Warhol

5. Vince Lombardi
6. Jacqueline Kennedy
7. Fred Flintstone
8. *Hill Street Blues*
9. Wendy's
10. Princess Diana
11. Ronald Reagan
12. Bill Clinton

Who's the Boss?
1. president
2. judge
3. teacher
4. principal
5. mayor
6. governor
7. captain
8. pilot, or captain
9. conductor
10. warden
11. captain
12. ensign

Who's the Boss? Bonus Questions
1. Jimmy Cagney
2. the director
3. *The Godfather*
4. *The Jetsons*
5. the conductor
6. the editor
7. the publisher
8. the police officer
9. Gordon Jump
10. Edward Asner
11. John O'Hurley
12. God

Will Rogers Sayings
1. town gossip
2. like
3. elected
4. subjects

5. somebody else
6. found out
7. lawyer
8. met the boat
9. repeat the facts
10. today
11. papers
12. for you

Will Rogers Sayings Bonus Questions
1. work
2. sunburned
3. them
4. rock
5. sit there
6. paying for
7. yourself
8. applesauce
9. Democrat
10. laugh
11. know
12. go by

William Shakespeare Quotes
1. crown
2. wit
3. are gone
4. lawyers
5. rain
6. child
7. circle
8. grease
9. purpose
10. smooth
11. monster
12. mortals be

William Shakespeare Quotes
  Bonus Questions
1. waste me
2. may be
3. thy head

4. nothing
5. kingdom
6. bubble
7. there
8. slept
9. mine
10. wink
11. fear
12. thy rest

Witches
1. witchcraft
2. *Bewitched*
3. Stevens
4. East
5. witch doctor
6. witch hazel
7. Salem, Massachusetts
8. witchcraft
9. Dorothy
10. *Candle*
11. a familiar
12. warlock

Yellow
1. yellow jacket
2. Kansas
3. goldenrod
4. a coward
5. yellow fever
6. "Yellow Submarine"
7. "Mellow Yellow"
8. …Yellow Polka-dot Bikini"
9. "Tie a Yellow Ribbon 'Round the Old Oak Tree"
10. "Big Yellow Taxi"
11. saffron
12. jaundice

Other Books by Venture Publishing, Inc.

21st Century Leisure: Current Issues, Second Edition
  by Valeria J. Freysinger and John R. Kelly
The A•B•Cs of Behavior Change: Skills for Working With Behavior Problems in Nursing Homes
  by Margaret D. Cohn, Michael A. Smyer, and Ann L. Horgas
Activity Experiences and Programming within Long-Term Care
  by Ted Tedrick and Elaine R. Green
The Activity Gourmet
  by Peggy Powers
Advanced Concepts for Geriatric Nursing Assistants
  by Carolyn A. McDonald
Adventure Programming
  edited by John C. Miles and Simon Priest
Assessment: The Cornerstone of Activity Programs
  by Ruth Perschbacher
Behavior Modification in Therapeutic Recreation: An Introductory Manual
  by John Datillo and William D. Murphy
Benefits of Leisure
  edited by B.L. Driver, Perry J. Brown, and George L. Peterson
Benefits of Recreation Research Update
  by Judy M. Sefton and W. Kerry Mummery
Beyond Baskets and Beads: Activities for Older Adults with Functional Impairments
  by Mary Hart, Karen Primm, and Kathy Cranisky
Beyond Bingo: Innovative Programs for the New Senior
  by Sal Arrigo, Jr., Ann Lewis, and Hank Mattimore
Beyond Bingo 2: More Innovative Programs for the New Senior
  by Sal Arrigo, Jr.
Boredom Busters: Themed Special Events to Dazzle and Delight Your Group
  by Annette C. Moore
Both Gains and Gaps: Feminist Perspectives on Women's Leisure
  by Karla Henderson, M. Deborah Bialeschki, Susan M. Shaw, and Valeria J. Freysinger
Client Assessment in Therapeutic Recreation Services
  by Norma J. Stumbo
Client Outcomes in Therapeutic Recreation Services
  by Norma J. Stumbo
Conceptual Foundations for Therapeutic Recreation
  edited by David R. Austin, John Dattilo, and Bryan P. McCormick
Constraints to Leisure
  edited by Edgar L. Jackson
Dementia Care Programming: An Identity-Focused Approach
  by Rosemary Dunne
Dimensions of Choice: Qualitative Approaches to Parks, Recreation, Tourism, Sport, and Leisure Research, Second Edition
  by Karla A. Henderson
Diversity and the Recreation Profession: Organizational Perspectives
  edited by Maria T. Allison and Ingrid E. Schneider
Effective Management in Therapeutic Recreation Service, Second Edition
  by Marcia Jean Carter and Gerald S. O'Morrow
Evaluating Leisure Services: Making Enlightened Decisions, Second Edition
  by Karla A. Henderson and M. Deborah Bialeschki

Everything from A to Y: The Zest Is up to You! Older Adult Activities for Every Day of the Year
   by Nancy R. Cheshire and Martha L. Kenney
The Evolution of Leisure: Historical and Philosophical Perspectives
   by Thomas Goodale and Geoffrey Godbey
Experience Marketing: Strategies for the New Millennium
   by Ellen L. O'Sullivan and Kathy J. Spangler
Facilitation Techniques in Therapeutic Recreation
   by John Dattilo
File o' Fun: A Recreation Planner for Games & Activities, Third Edition
   by Jane Harris Ericson and Diane Ruth Albright
Functional Interdisciplinary-Transdisciplinary Therapy (FITT) Manual
   by Deborah M. Schott, Judy D. Burdett, Beverly J. Cook, Karren S. Ford, and
   Kathleen M. Orban
The Game and Play Leader's Handbook: Facilitating Fun and Positive Interaction, Revised Edition
   by Bill Michaelis and John M. O'Connell
The Game Finder—A Leader's Guide to Great Activities
   by Annette C. Moore
Getting People Involved in Life and Activities: Effective Motivating Techniques
   by Jeanne Adams
Glossary of Recreation Therapy and Occupational Therapy
   by David R. Austin
Great Special Events and Activities
   by Annie Morton, Angie Prosser, and Sue Spangler
Group Games & Activity Leadership
   by Kenneth J. Bulik
Growing With Care: Using Greenery, Gardens, and Nature With Aging and Special Populations
   by Betsy Kreidler
Hands On! Children's Activities for Fairs, Festivals, and Special Events
   by Karen L. Ramey
Health Promotion for Mind, Body and Spirit
   by Suzanne Fitzsimmons and Linda L. Buettner
In Search of the Starfish: Creating a Caring Environment
   by Mary Hart, Karen Primm, and Kathy Cranisky
Inclusion: Including People With Disabilities in Parks and Recreation Opportunities
   by Lynn Anderson and Carla Brown Kress
Inclusive Leisure Services: Responding to the Rights of People with Disabilities, Second Edition
   by John Dattilo
Innovations: A Recreation Therapy Approach to Restorative Programs
   by Dawn R. De Vries and Julie M. Lake
Internships in Recreation and Leisure Services: A Practical Guide for Students, Third Edition
   by Edward E. Seagle, Jr. and Ralph W. Smith
Interpretation of Cultural and Natural Resources, Second Edition
   by Douglas M. Knudson, Ted T. Cable, and Larry Beck
Intervention Activities for At-Risk Youth
   by Norma J. Stumbo
Introduction to Outdoor Recreation: Providing and Managing Resource Based Opportunities
   by Roger L. Moore and B.L. Driver
Introduction to Recreation and Leisure Services, Eighth Edition
   by Karla A. Henderson, M. Deborah Bialeschki, John L. Hemingway, Jan S. Hodges,
   Beth D. Kivel, and H. Douglas Sessoms

Outdoor Recreation Management: Theory and Application, Third Edition
    by Alan Jubenville and Ben Twight
Parks for Life: Moving the Goal Posts, Changing the Rules, and Expanding the Field
    by Will LaPage
Planning and Organizing Group Activities in Social Recreation
    by John V. Valentine
Planning Parks for People, Second Edition
    by John Hultsman, Richard L. Cottrell, and Wendy Z. Hultsman
The Process of Recreation Programming Theory and Technique, Third Edition
    by Patricia Farrell and Herberta M. Lundegren
Programming for Parks, Recreation, and Leisure Services: A Servant Leadership Approach,
Second Edition
    by Debra J. Jordan, Donald G. DeGraaf, and Kathy H. DeGraaf
Protocols for Recreation Therapy Programs
    edited by Jill Kelland, along with the Recreation Therapy Staff at Alberta Hospital Edmonton
Puttin' on the Skits: Plays for Adults in Managed Care
    by Jean Vetter
Quality Management: Applications for Therapeutic Recreation
    edited by Bob Riley
A Recovery Workbook: The Road Back from Substance Abuse
    by April K. Neal and Michael J. Taleff
Recreation and Leisure: Issues in an Era of Change, Third Edition
    edited by Thomas Goodale and Peter A. Witt
Recreation and Youth Development
    by Peter A. Witt and Linda L. Caldwell
Recreation Economic Decisions: Comparing Benefits and Costs, Second Edition
    by John B. Loomis and Richard G. Walsh
Recreation for Older Adults: Individual and Group Activities
    by Judith A. Elliott and Jerold E. Elliott
Recreation Program Planning Manual for Older Adults
    by Karen Kindrachuk
Recreation Programming and Activities for Older Adults
    by Jerold E. Elliott and Judith A. Sorg-Elliott
Reference Manual for Writing Rehabilitation Therapy Treatment Plans
    by Penny Hogberg and Mary Johnson
Research in Therapeutic Recreation: Concepts and Methods
    edited by Marjorie J. Malkin and Christine Z. Howe
Simple Expressions: Creative and Therapeutic Arts for the Elderly in Long-Term Care Facilities
    by Vicki Parsons
A Social History of Leisure Since 1600
    by Gary Cross
A Social Psychology of Leisure
    by Roger C. Mannell and Douglas A. Kleiber
Special Events and Festivals: How to Organize, Plan, and Implement
    by Angie Prosser and Ashli Rutledge
Stretch Your Mind and Body: Tai Chi as an Adaptive Activity
    by Duane A. Crider and William R. Klinger
Therapeutic Activity Intervention with the Elderly: Foundations and Practices
    by Barbara A. Hawkins, Marti E. May, and Nancy Brattain Rogers
Therapeutic Recreation and the Nature of Disabilities
    by Kenneth E. Mobily and Richard D. MacNeil

Therapeutic Recreation: Cases and Exercises, Second Edition
  by Barbara C. Wilhite and M. Jean Keller
Therapeutic Recreation in Health Promotion and Rehabilitation
  by John Shank and Catherine Coyle
Therapeutic Recreation in the Nursing Home
  by Linda Buettner and Shelley L. Martin
Therapeutic Recreation Programming: Theory and Practice
  by Charles Sylvester, Judith E. Voelkl, and Gary D. Ellis
Therapeutic Recreation Protocol for Treatment of Substance Addictions
  by Rozanne W. Faulkner
The Therapeutic Recreation Stress Management Primer
  by Cynthia Mascott
The Therapeutic Value of Creative Writing
  by Paul M. Spicer
Tourism and Society: A Guide to Problems and Issues
  by Robert W. Wyllie
Traditions: Improving Quality of Life in Caregiving
  by Janelle Sellick

Venture Publishing, Inc.
1999 Cato Avenue
State College, PA 16801
Phone: 814-234-4561
Fax: 814-234-1651